Translation of

Khurbn Czenstochow

Destruction of Czenstochow (Częstochowa, Poland)

Originally in Yiddish

By Shlomo Waga

Translated and Edited by Gloria Berkenstat Freund

Published by JewishGen

**An Affiliate of the Museum of Jewish Heritage
A Living Memorial to the Holocaust**

Khurbn Czenstochow
Destruction of Czenstochow

Translated by Gloria Berkenstat Freund

Copyright © 2012 by Gloria Berkenstat Freund
All rights reserved.
First Printing: January 2012, Shevat 5772
Second Printing: March 2019, Adar II 5779

Editors: Gloria Berkenstat Freund and Joel Alpert
Layout: Joel Alpert
Image Editor: Jan R. Fine
Cover Design: Jan R. Fine
Publicity: Sandra Hirschhorn

Published by JewishGen, Inc.
An Affiliate of the Museum of Jewish Heritage
A Living Memorial to the Holocaust
36 Battery Place, New York, NY 10280

"JewishGen, Inc. is not responsible for inaccuracies or omissions in the original work and makes no representations regarding the accuracy of this translation. Digital images of the original book's contents can be seen online at the New York Public Library Web site."

The mission of the JewishGen organization is to produce a translation of the original work and we cannot verify the accuracy of statements or alter facts cited.

Printed in the United States of America by Lightning Source, Inc.

Library of Congress Control Number (LCCN): 2012930458
ISBN: 978-0-9764759-5-8 (hard cover: 200 pages, alk. paper)

Cover photograph: From the cover of the original Yiddish book

JewishGen and the Yizkor Books in Print Project

This book has been published by the **Yizkor Books in Print Project,** as part of the **Yizkor Book Project** of JewishGen, Inc.

JewishGen, Inc. is a non-profit organization founded in 1987 as a resource for Jewish genealogy. Its website [www.jewishgen.org] serves as an international clearinghouse and resource center to assist individuals who are researching the history of their Jewish families and the places where they lived. JewishGen provides databases, facilitates discussion groups, and coordinates projects relating to Jewish genealogy and the history of the Jewish people. In 2003, JewishGen became an affiliate of the **Museum of Jewish Heritage - A Living Memorial to the Holocaust** in New York.

The **JewishGen Yizkor Book Project** was organized to make more widely known the existence of Yizkor (Memorial) Books written by survivors and former residents of various Jewish communities throughout the world. Later, volunteers connected to the different destroyed communities began cooperating to have these books translated from the original language—usually Hebrew or Yiddish—into English, thus enabling a wider audience to have access to the valuable information contained within them. As each chapter of these books was translated, it was posted on the JewishGen website and made available to the general public.

The **Yizkor Books in Print Project** began in 2011 as an initiative to print and publish Yizkor Books that had been fully translated, so that hard copies would be available for purchase by the descendants of these communities and also by scholars, universities, synagogues, libraries, and museums.

These Yizkor books have been produced almost entirely through the volunteer effort of researchers from around the world, assisted by donations from private individuals. The books are printed and sold at near cost, so as to make them as affordable as possible. Our goal is to make this important genre of Jewish literature and history available in English in book form, so that people can have the personal histories of their ancestral towns on their bookshelves for themselves and for their children and grandchildren.

Lance Ackerfeld, Yizkor Book Project Manager

Joel Alpert, Yizkor Book in Print Project Coordinator

Yiddish Title Page of Original Yiddish Book

שלמה וואגא

חורבן טשענסטאכאוו

ornament

אַרויסגעגעבן דורכן
צענטראל פאַרבאַנד פון פוילישע יידן אין אַרגענטינע
צוזאַמען מיטן
טשענסטאַכאָווער לאנדם ־ לייט פאַריין אין אַרגענטינע
בוענאָס איירעס 1949

Translation of the Title Page of Original Yiddish Book

Shlomo Waga

KHURBN CZENSTOCHOW

☙

Published by

Central Union of Polish Jews in Argentina

Together with

Czenstochower *Landsleit* Union in Argentina

Buenos Aires 1949

ביבער־סעריע

דאָס פּױלישע ײדנטום

46

רעדאקטאר:

מארק טורקאװ

פארלאג־לייטער:

אברהם מיטלבערג

די רשימה פון דערשינענע בענד — צום סוף פונעם בוך

In Original Yiddish Book

PRINTED IN ARGENTINE
IMPRESSO EN LA ARGENTINA

S. Waga

CHURBN CZENSTOCHOW

(Destrucción de Chenstojowa)

Buenos Aires 1949

Hecho el despósito que march la Ley 11.732
Industria Argentina

This book was published on the 20th of April 1949
by the Heuman Publishers – Pasteur 333
Telephone 47-7752 – Buenos Aires

Forward for the Translation

This translation has its origins in Israel in 2004, when I met my cousin David Berkenstadt for the first time. As we were saying goodbye, he handed me a tattered book, *Hurbn Czenstochow*. Back home in New York, I began to translate the Yiddish text into English, a task that took me about two years.

My interest in Czestochowa had two sources: the first is the fact that my beloved Uncle Harry Jacobs (Hershlik Jakubowicz) was born there; the second is that many of my Berkensztat relatives spent their lives and met their tragic deaths in that city, as did my Uncle Harry's family. My interest in translating the book came from the fact that the events in the book are what they experienced. The world must not forget what happened to them. I hope others with ancestral connections to Czestochowa will find this book useful in understanding what their family members endured. It is important to make the information contained in the book available to English readers who cannot read the Yiddish text.

Gloria Berkenstat Freund
Translator and Project Coordinator

Dedication in Original Yiddish Book

Dedication

This book about the destruction of our
birthplace
Czenstochow is dedicated to the sacred memory
of:

My father Yakov Zwi Waga
My mother Bajla Gitl Waga
My brother Moshe and his wife Chana Waga
As well as their children Surale and Chawale
Waga

Who were annihilated by the Germans.

The Author, S. Waga

Acknowledgements for the Translation

Thank you to the JewishGen organization for making possible both the on-line publication and the publication of this hardcover edition of this translation.

The translation and production of this book would not have been possible without the help of the following very generous people:

David Berkenstadt of Haifa, my cousin, who so kindly made this book available for translation.

Pesakh Fiszman, of blessed memory, my incomparable Yiddish teacher, who taught me so well and encouraged me in my love of Yiddish and *Yiddishkeit.*

Larry Freund, my beloved husband, who selflessly read and reread my translation and shared his editing skills with me.

Joyce Field, Emerita Yizkor Book Project Manager, who provided me with encouragement throughout the translation process.

Lance Ackerfeld, JewishGen Yizkor Book Project Manager, who made sure that the translation reached the JewishGen Yizkor Book Translation Project website.

Joel Alpert, Yizkor Books in Print Project Coordinator, who also did the layout of this book.

Jan R. Fine, Image Editor, who took my scans of the often fuzzy photographs in the book and gave them clarity.

Gloria Berkenstat Freund
Translator and Project Coordinator

Notes to the Reader:

Please note that the page number in the original Yiddish book is indicated by: "**p. 9**" on the left-hand side of the page. This will enable the reader to go to the original book for reference and verification of translation from the Yiddish. When the text of paragraphs were split between a page and the succeeding page in the original book, the editor of the translation took the liberty of placing the section of the paragraph from the succeeding page onto the preceding page in this translation to make it more readable and neater.

The name of the town can be spelled as Czestochowa, Czenstochowa and many other ways.

This is a translation from: Khurbn Czenstochow, (The Destruction of Czenstochow) Editor: S. Waga,

Publisher: Tsentral-farband fun Poylishe Yidn in Buenos Aires, Argentine, 1949 (Yiddish)

Note: As of the date of the publication of this translation, the original book can be seen online at the NY Public Library at:
http://yizkor.nypl.org/index.php?id=1887

JewishGen
Yizkor Book Project

This book is presented by the
Yizkor Books in Print Project
Project Coordinator: Joel Alpert

Part of the
Yizkor Books Project of JewishGen, Inc.
Project Manager: Lance Ackerfeld

These books have been produced solely through volunteer effort of individuals from around the world. The books are printed and sold at near cost, so as to make them as affordable as possible

Our goal is to make this history and important genre of Jewish literature available in English in book form so that people can have the near-personal histories of their ancestral towns on their bookshelves for themselves and for their children and grandchildren

Any donations to the Yizkor Books Project are appreciated

Please send donations to:
Yizkor Book Project
JewishGen
36 Battery Place
New York, NY 10280

·

JewishGen, Inc. is an affiliate of the
Museum of Jewish Heritage
A Living Memorial to the Holocaust

Table of Contents

p. 9

Chapter I

The Germans in Czenstochow

It was already clear on the first day of the war, Friday, the 1st of September 1939, that the Germans would occupy Czenstochow. With shocking strength, they faced the Polish troops that were diverted deep into the country.

The entire population was engulfed in a mood of panic and began to follow the retreat of the army, abandoning everything. The last trains and private autos that went in the direction of Warsaw, Kielce and other cities were full of people.

Escaping still farther was the only thought of the people who were filled with fear of the arriving Germans.

Friday night thousands of peasants and their families from the surrounding villages marched through the city on foot and in wagons with their cows and everything they could take with them.

The highways and roads were so overflowing with wandering masses of people that the retreating Polish army had to make a great effort in order to break through a road for its further retreat.

p. 10

The German airplanes immediately appeared over the highways, descended, and shot the panicked, escaping people with machine guns. They abandoned their possessions, their cattle, in order to save their own lives. The dead fell and covered the roads of those escaping.

When the last Polish army division left Czenstochow, the bridges were ripped out and the city was cut off for those who later wanted to leave.

Sunday, the third day of the war, at ten in the morning, the first advance positions and patrols appeared in the city and went through the streets with tanks. There was beautiful, summery weather. The alarmed population began to look out through the windows with great caution and, seeing that it was quiet, slowly, and unsure, went out on the streets.

Little by little the individual German military men approached the civilians, carried on conversations with them, even with the Jews.

The same day, in the afternoon hours, large divisions of German troops appeared in the city. Many of them went into private homes to wash and drink a little water.

The population immediately was aware that the city was under German occupation and there was a mood of depression.

p. 11

Chapter II

Bloody Monday

Monday, in the morning, on the fourth day of the war, the first German decree that all of the businesses should be opened immediately was published. The residents of the city began to move through the streets. Suddenly, the passersby drew back at seeing the way the German troops with pointed guns were leading a large group of people with hands raised in the air under heavy guard. Many of the people were half-dressed. This image made a distressing impression on everyone, because it became clear the terror was beginning.

Two hours later, while in my residence, I heard shooting that grew stronger with each minute. Everyone was seized by fear. Suddenly, we heard a knock on our door and someone desperately calling out:

"Have mercy! Let us in!"

We immediately opened the door and several Jews entered our residence who told us that the Germans were chasing after people and shooting at those going by. It did not take long until the Germans broke into private residences and drove everyone out on the street.

They did not omit our apartment. Knocking on the doors with rifle butts, they asked to be let in. When I opened the door, they entered the apartment and the order of a soldier was given:

Hands up, everyone out!

We were hurriedly driven out to the courtyard where our neighbors already were and we were led out to the street, being driven just as the people we had seen on the street in the morning.

p. 12

The streets were full of troops. Their weapons were aimed in our direction and when our eyes met theirs, they laughed in our faces. When they recognized a Jew, they hit him over the head with a rifle butt.

Marching through the streets, we met other groups that were also driven out of their homes.

Immediately, they began to sort us – men separately and women separately. The Germans counted 200 people from our group and, forcing us constantly to hold our hands up, quickly drove us to the city managing committee building. German military men with machine guns in their hands were already waiting for us near large trenches that had been dug and were supposed to serve as air raid shelters. One of them called out loudly:

– There they are, the dogs, all will soon be shot and they will be thrown in the trenches....

A fear engulfed us. Because of tiredness, we could no longer hold our hands in the air; they fell on our heads. We asked each other, barely moving our lips, are these our last minutes.... Some of the people recited Psalms silently.

Here, the following characteristic episode that happened during those frightening minutes on that spot must be remembered: a young Jewish man of about 31, standing with all of us in the line, shook terribly and, therefore, urine began to pour from his pants. This was noticed by one of the officers who stood near us. He moved closer to the young man and asked him:

p. 13

– Why are you shaking, swine? Now you are afraid... Why did you shoot our troops?

Hearing such words, we all immediately understood where we stood in the world. Our thoughts were quickly interrupted when a Pole, who stood in our line, suddenly called to the officer in broken German:

– *Verflukhter Yude* [Cursed Jew], he is guilty, we are innocent...

However, the officer quickly calmed him:

– We will be finished soon with the Jews...

After holding us in a standing position under the burning sun the entire two hours time, not letting us move from the spot, ten military men came out of the building of the city managing committee and began to search every one of us. Whoever had a shaving knife with them, a pocket knife or other sharp things, had to jump immediately into the trenches that were surrounded by troops who constantly shot at the people in the trenches.

If someone did not have something sharp with him, his fate hung with the military man who searched him: did he please the military man or not. Choosing people for death was done so quickly that rows of people awaiting death had already formed near the pits. The people watching the way the executions occurred, wrung their hands, tore their hair and flung themselves to the ground shouting and calling for help with their last strength.

p. 14

I stood in the middle of a group and waited to be searched. Some secret strength pushed me from the line; I went to a German, whose appearance seemed to me to be a little kinder. I unbuttoned my coat, took everything out that I had in my pockets, a lead pencil, a pen, a wallet, a handkerchief and giving everything to the German, I said to him:

– See, I have nothing more with me. However, I left my old parents, a wife and a child at home who cannot live without me.

The German looked at me and told me to stand on the left, that is, among those who would be allowed to live. I breathed easier.

Standing this way in the saved group, with my hands in the air and with my face to the pit, where the first Czenstochowers were martyred, I noticed how the Pole who had denounced the trembling Jew in our row, was being pushed into the pit and a German immediately shot him. In contrast, the shaking young man was placed in the saved group.

The religious young man did not himself believe his luck and said:

– God took pity on me and punished the villain who denounced me...

Barely a third of the people, who were driven to the pits with us, survived.

In the interim, new groups of people, whose faith was the same as our groups, were brought from various parts of the city.

p.15

Who knows how long the executions would have been carried out, when an air alarm and shooting at the Polish airplanes that appeared over the city had not suddenly been heard. The Germans ordered everyone to lie on the ground. The German soldiers did the same thing, lying on the ground with their guns aimed in our direction. Then there was an order:

– If anyone moves from their spot or lifts their head they will immediately be shot.

We tried to bury our heads in the earth. The shooting became stronger and stronger. The bullets literally flew over our bodies and we were sure that we would not emerge alive. Jews called, *"Shema Yisroel"* [the central prayer of Judaism stating that God is one] and recited Psalms. The Christians also called to their sacred ones for help.

Everyone trembled with fear that the Germans would hear the prayers and be disturbed by them.

When the shooting, which lasted a long time, finally ceased, we were ordered to stand up and were told to go in the direction of the stalls where the horses were. However, not everyone stood up. There were dead in our group.

Tired, we fell upon the horse dirt in the stalls and fell asleep. The Germans locked the stalls.

The mass execution that we attended was not the only one in the city. The Germans arranged similar executions in various parts of the city, including the courtyard of the Jewish craft workers school at Garncarska 19. Similar hunts also took place in the churches, synagogues and in all public premises and places with similar executions involving Czenstochower residents.

p. 16

Entire houses were set on fire and burned with the inhabitants, who were not allowed to leave. If someone tried to jump out of a window of a burning house, he was immediately shot.

The Germans set up machine guns across the entire city and, without warning, the soldiers shot at everyone who appeared on the streets.

Thus the first bloody Monday passed in Czenstochow.

Chapter III

Under the Nazi Yoke

The Germans first came into our stall late at night. The old people were permitted to go home and the young, hungry, tired and thirsty were driven through the dead streets like horrible criminals under heavy military guard. No one was permitted to speak, but had to march silently until we arrived at the military barracks, *Zowada*. We were held for a long time on the shooting range, in order to throw a fear in us that we would be executed. Finally, we were taken to the cellars under the barracks.

As we went down to the cellar, we felt ourselves being shoved down the stairs, pressed together in a mass, one on the other. It was pitch dark and we saw nothing. Coming down, we heard human voices, which we took as a sign that someone else was there.

p. 17

Through the small cellar windows, we heard the Germans coercing other people, hitting and cursing them in a vulgar way.

The cellar in which we were held was very low and our heads touched the ceiling. It was stuffy and we could not catch our breath. Therefore, everyone pushed to open windows. The old and the sick fell to the ground half unconscious and groaning. After a certain time, someone accidentally stumbled upon a water faucet that was located in the cellar, opened it and sprayed himself with water. Our joy could not be expressed. The group pushed toward the faucet with hands, hats, and caps in order to refresh their hearts with a little water. Finally, the day began. People looked at one another, began to speak among themselves and made an account of the number of victims on the bloody Monday. It was estimated that 5,000 innocent human lives perished.

At dawn, the Germans immediately let us feel that Jews belong to a lower category of human species. The soldier, who guarded us near the door, yelled loudly:

– Four Jews go out and clean the courtyard! At that, he said that all of the Jews had to work from today on and, therefore, requested that the Jews voluntarily report to work. Seeing that no one voluntarily reported, the soldier declared that no one should be afraid, nothing bad would happen to anyone. Then, several Jews volunteered to work and a while later, through the small windows, we saw them clearing the courtyard.

The Peretz House (Photograph by A. Kocyzna)

The German Shul (Photograph by A. Kocyzna)

p. 18

The time in the cellar stretched into boredom and hunger was strongly felt. At 11 o'clock, the German soldier began calling out several of us by our family names. It turned out that wives and relatives of those detained had looked for us all over the city, wanting to give us something to eat. Alas, there were many wives who had to return home with their packages of food because those for whom they were looking were already dead.

I finally heard my name called out during the day at one. I quickly ran up the steps and saw my wife and child. We cried with joy that we finally were seeing each other. However, the joy did not last long. The soldier drove me right back into the cellar. The mood was a little excited because we had seen those closest to us and we could eat to our satisfaction. The relationships in the cellar were comradely. Food was shared with those whose relatives had not come with packages.

In the morning, at 11 o'clock, we received an order to leave the cellar and to stand in the courtyard in rows. We were immediately taken to the large exercise space near the barracks and there we met the gigantic mass of people who were brought here from our cellar.

We stood this way under the burning sun for several hours until we were told the good news that we would be freed because the factories would be activated, the shops must again be opened and the economic life in the city must be renewed. Therefore, all of those who were industrialists, high officials, *gymnazie* [high school] professors, lawyers, doctors and, in general, all of those who were important in communal life, were asked to leave the rows. These people would be freed first and then later the rest would be freed.

p. 19

A large number of those indicated left the rows and stood in the designated spot. I also stood there waiting for them to free us shortly.

The officers looked over our papers and chose 50 people who were asked to stand on the side. The remainder were sent back to their earlier places among the large mass of people, berated that they did not mean them, only actual industrial and learned people. I remained among the 50 chosen. We were taken to a tennis court that was surrounded with a high wire fence and at the entrance stood an armed soldier who would not permit anyone to enter or exit the fences.

The large mass of people was envious of us. A number of them even wanted to join us. They insisted to the soldier on guard, showing their documents, that one is a lawyer, another a doctor, this one a high ministerial official from Warsaw who got stuck in Czenstochow by accident. Tailors declared that they were confectionary manufacturers, shoemakers were shoe manufacturers, traders wanted to present themselves as large merchants with their tax office registration cards – everyone wanted to join our group.

A friend of mine, an engineer, a well known worker, stood on the other side of the barbed wire and begged me to have pity on him and to ensure that he joined our group because he was sick and would not last if he was not freed immediately. I went to the soldier, tried to show him that my friend, the engineer, was an important specialist. However, the soldier answered me that I must talk to the lieutenant, who would be coming soon about this.

p. 20

My friend was not satisfied with the answer and with the help of a piece of iron he began to dig the ground from under the fence. I helped him with the work from inside the fence and, after 20 minutes, my friend was able to crawl on his stomach to me.

When the officer came to the spot he permitted some people to join us on the tennis court. The new arrivals – just like me – felt happy, being sure that shortly we would be going home.

Meanwhile, we saw how some officers came to the spot; lined up the large group again in rows and with the intercession of an interpreter, the officers told the crowd that there would be no resistance to the Germans, everyone must remain calm, follow all orders, work well and not engage in politics. A signal was given and the entire group marched past the officers in rows and taking off their hat to them, everyone had to say: "We thank you, we thank you."

We stood near the barbed wire of the tennis court like animals in a cage and saw how the multitude continued to leave the barracks area. But from each group that left, an officer selected a tall person and let him join us.

Since everyone was going home, yet new people were being allowed to join us, we became very uneasy, particularly because those newly permitted to join us had no connection, not with any industry and not with the earlier professions. Our entire group was assembled near the guarded entrance to the tennis court, so that we could be permitted to go home.

The hours moved ahead and it was already 6 at night. The giant space around us that hours before had been flooded with many thousands of people was now completely empty. My friend, the engineer, was terribly nervous. What had he done? He could have already been at home and here we did not know what would happen to us.

p. 21

Suddenly, we saw six German officers, one civilian and someone in the uniform of a Polish non-commissioned officer approaching us. They came to us in the fenced off tennis court. We watched them with frightened looks as we awaited our fate. An order was heard that we should stand in two rows and the Polish non-commissioned officer came to each of us and wrote our names in a book.

During this incident, 50 new Jews were led into the tennis court. They were heavily guarded and held their hands in the air. When the non-commissioned officer was finished with us, he also recorded the names of the new arrivals and then the Jews were separated from the Christians into distinct groups.

When these formalities were finished, the man dressed in civilian clothes approached us with an expression full of hate on his face and gave the following talk in Polish:

– I and my colleague – here, he pointed to the Polish non-commissioned officer – and our colleagues, other Poles, too, for a long time we watched how everything appeared when you – here he turned in our direction – Jews and your government abandoned the country. You did not give the Polish population the means to live; the workers and the peasants lived in desolation and need during the time when you ran your businesses with great earnings for yourselves, paying the workers and office workers hunger wages. You promoted your people to the highest state offices, in order to carry out your plans through them. You influenced the government to enact laws that would be for your benefit. And when we "Aryans" spoke up in the *Sejm*, in order to defend ourselves against your rule, you immediately raised an alarm throughout the world that we want to annihilate you. You sent delegations to America asking that they not give us money. You did everything in order to disturb the development of the Polish state. All of the people who were gathered in this place last night and today had to work for you for tens of years. They were your slaves. We, the true Polish patriots, could not watch your rule over the Polish people indifferently and, therefore, it will be better to have the Germans...

p. 22

Then he turned to the gathered Poles:

– You Poles did not understand all of this. You helped the Jews in Poland and also in other countries so that they could devise plans with their governments to surround present day Germany on all sides. You did not want to understand that in the end a person would appear in the world who would govern the German people in the name of justice and with the right program, a person who defeated the Jews in Germany and, hopefully, would do that here...

And again he turned toward us:

- You *Zides* [pejorative Polish word for Jews] depicted the great leader of the German people, Adolf Hitler, as a pig in various playthings and made fun of him...

Hearing the name, Adolf Hitler, one of the German officers immediately turned to the speaker asking what he had said. The speaker told the officer in German that on many of the streets in Polish cities the Jews would sell playthings in the form of a painted handkerchief that when folded together presented Hitler in the caricature of a pig.

p. 23

The officers became furious and they moved closer to our group with balled fists, screaming with anger:

- We will show you who we are! Do not think that we are the Germans who came here in 1914...

The oldest officer did not let the Polish civilian end his sermon, but told us in a sharp and categorical tone:

- From now on you are our hostages. If something bad happens to a German, civilian or military man, caused by the local population, you will immediately be shot and the entire garbage will be burned! – He ended pointing his finger to the city.

Two young men fainted during the venomous talk of the Polish civilian. The soldiers would not let them get up from the ground. One officer said with hate:

- Let them die!

* *
*

With heavy spirits and tired, we could barely move from the spot. With our heads down, not uttering one word to each other, we let ourselves be taken by the soldier guards deep into the courtyard of the barracks, then into a sort of dark corridor until we were led to a room and the door was locked from outside.

The room was large. It was a repair shop for ammunition. Long tables and large cabinets stood around the walls. There was also a water faucet.

In addition to our group that was brought from the tennis court, there was another group in the room that had been brought directly from the city. A rabbi from our neighborhood was found among this group. He was dressed in his long silk caftan and a wide hat. Pious Jews moved toward him, paid for advice and asked for help. The rabbi told each Jew to make a vow that he would immediately fulfill upon gaining freedom. He also said to recite prayers and to atone. He consoled everyone and said to have reliance in God who would and must help. The pious Jews were encouraged and strengthened by the rabbi's consoling words. It unquestionably became easier for them than for the non-believers.

p. 24

The Polish non-commissioned officer came in early in the morning with two German officers, told us to stand in a row and called out the names of one group and they freed them all. Several who complained of their bad health were also freed. Among those freed were Jews and Poles. The German officer declared at the freeing that if anything happens in the city, all of the hostages would immediately be shot.

Fifty of us remained, of whom 35 were Jews and 15 Poles. We devoted ourselves to a clear accounting of the great burden that fell on us, that our lives hung on the incidents in the city. Our mood was pessimistic because we knew very well that with the smallest provocation, the Germans would immediately annihilate us. We simply could not understand why the number of Jewish hostages was so large in proportion to the Poles at a time when the Jewish population in the city was only about 20 percent.

The deliberations and conversations among us were interrupted when a military guard appeared in the room and told us all to leave because the women were coming with food. Encountering those closest to us brought out great joy. They had waited for six hours at the barracks until they were finally allowed to come to us. We wanted to be informed about the situation in the city, about the fate of our relatives and acquaintances. With luck, the city was quiet. The military guard moved among us with loaded revolvers in their hands, carefully searching the baskets of food that had been brought to us and, after a short time, the women were told to go home.

p. 25

When we came back to the big room, we could see that the Christian hostages had been separated from us. The commandant ordered this so that the "Aryans" would not be placed together with the Jews.

In the middle of the night we were awakened by a loud noise in the courtyard and the light from reflectors. We left our uncomfortable beds quickly and ran to the windows to see what was happening.

A row of trucks packed with people appeared before our eyes. The soldiers forced the people out of the trucks, beating them with rifle butts. Screaming was heard and the coerced and beaten people called out the names of Christian saints. Many of the people were half naked. There was a great deal of movement by the trucks. The empty trucks drove away and new ones fully packed with people arrived. The shooting became more frequent and the screaming louder. Those being coerced ran behind each other, and were lit from all sides by the strong reflectors. They were beaten and coerced from all sides.

We first learned in the morning that those people who had been brought had been caught on the highways where they had wandered to escape from the war operations.

p. 26

Eight Jews were taken from our group and they were driven out of the courtyard. We became very alarmed at first about their fate, but later, through a window, we saw that they were cleaning the large courtyard of the dead bodies of those shot. Dozens of victims were carried out on plain boards to somewhere behind the walls of the barracks.

This work lasted several hours. When our comrades came back, they were tired from the work and gathered together. We gave them the name *khevre-kadishe yidn* [burial society Jews].

Three days passed in constant waiting and constant unease. Our only consolation was the families who would bring us food and of whom we would ask about what was happening in the city.

At night on the third day, soldiers came to us and led out 10 young people. This threw a fear on us. However, they came back after two hours and told us they had carried straw for the soldiers. Therefore, we suffered only from fear.

Chapter IV

Again Fear of Death

The subsequent days stretched as heavy as lead and full of painful waiting for us in our barracks jail. If there was a calm day for us, soon we again had the earlier *gehinim* [hell] on another day.

Every day, the military in the barracks would change. After spending the night, the military divisions would leave and in their place came new ones.

p. 27

It would happen that the Austrian or Czechoslovak military would arrive. Then the attitude toward us on the part of the soldiers was more human, as opposed to the forces that came from Germany, who treated us brutally and tortured us at every opportunity.

Once, late at night, several military men came to us, shined flashlights in our faces and asked each of us: "What are you?"

The answers came:

"Manufacturer, doctor, lawyer." Only one of the Jews with a long beard answered the posed question, "watchmaker." In this way, they asked each one and then went into a nearby room where the Poles were. They returned to us in about 15 minutes and one of them stood in the middle of the room and said:

– I am the Commandant of the city. I warn you, you dreadful Jews, that if any crime occurs in the city against we Germans, we will stand you all against the wall.

They left with heavy steps and the door was locked.

None of us slept for the rest of the night. Fear engulfed us all. We devoted ourselves to making an accounting of the weapons that hung over us.

In the morning, when we began to climb down from the tables after a sleepless night, a sergeant major came in to us and said:

– Tonight, two non-commissioned officers did not return from the city. When your wives come to you with breakfast, you should tell them that if our two men are not found by 12 noon, we will shoot you.

The news reached us like thunder. We were all scared to death and when the door opened later and the order was given: "Everyone out!" that we should go for breakfast, which had been brought earlier by our wives – several did not want to go to get their food in order to avoid having to tell their own family members such bitter news. Even now, however, each of us was driven out to the tennis court with shouts and force.

p. 28

There was a great wail when our wives heard the news. Several enrobed themselves in strength and went to the commandant. However, they returned immediately even more desperate: he had repeated the same thing for them that he had told us several hours earlier. The time arrived when the wives had to leave us and the separation this time was worse than before. Children cried bitterly, wives fainted and military personnel who were watching this scene gave mocking looks, making cutting movements with their fingers across their throats and yelled: "Your road is coming soon!" That meant they would soon make an end of us.

Our closest ones had to leave us and we were led back to the barracks hall under stronger guard. The soldiers that we encountered along the way pelted us with curses and threatened us with their fists. Apparently, the military in the barracks knew everything. Our guards only just brought us back to the barracks hall in one piece.

We entered our jail hall broken and desperate; no one touched the packages of food that had been brought. If the two soldiers were not found – everything was over. However there was one man who reacted differently from everyone else. This was the manufacturer, Gershon Preger of blessed memory, well known in Czenstochow. On the tennis court, too, during the tragic scenes, when everyone said goodbye to their wife as if for the last time, he and his wife absolutely did not want to speak about what awaited us. Returning to the hall, he sat down at the table as usual and began to eat. After finishing and cleaning the table, as he would always do, he turned to us with these words:

p. 29

– None of us has the strength to change our situation. Therefore, we must accept things as they come. I will live as long as I have been given, and I believe that this is not dependent on the assassins who will annihilate me, but from what kind of fate is ordained for me.

We were all envious of his determined character.

The Poles in the neighboring room lived through the same fear of death as we; they begged the soldier who guarded them for help in getting a priest before the execution. The soldier gave [the request] to the office. However, a refusal came from there.

The door opened at 11:30 and two soldiers entered. Everyone instinctively moved further from the door into the room, wanting to avoid being the first taken to be executed. The soldiers came deeper into the room to where we were all pressed together and called out to us:

– You are lucky, our comrades are here. Meanwhile, nothing will happen to you.

We all breathed easier, as if a heavy stone was taken off our heart. Our joy was still greater when we again came together with our wives at the tennis court. They had already received the good news from the soldier guard at the gate; some learned in the city that the two soldiers had been found. They were, as it was learned, with prostitutes the entire night. Meanwhile, we were saved. Tears of joy were shown even by our cold-blooded comrade. He was correct that we would live as long as was preordained.

p. 30

Chapter V

Looting and Sadism

We knew that the German regime was taking over private houses in the city for themselves. Tenants were being thrown out and various offices were being established there. In addition the Germans were taking all of the Jewish residences, which the residents had left. The rich Jewish residences were looted; linen, furniture and everything left was taken. It was also known that one Jew who they had today thrown out of his apartment had been ordered to create a representative group of several people who would give the orders of the German regime to the Jewish population.

Ten days had already passed since the Germans had entered the city. They were a frightening ten days and nights.

The barracks were full of people. The divisions that arrived rested for 24 hours and went farther away, apparently to the front. The soldiers loved to stop near our windows and tease us. They pointed to their guns, ready to shoot at us. We saw various types here. One would simply start a conversation about the blood that Jews drip from their ears; another – about Jewish wealth at the expense of the "Aryan" peoples and still other Hitlerist themes. We hid the watchmaker with the long beard from their eyes. However, one of the soldiers noticed this Jew and demanded that he come to the window. The German began arguing with the Jew about the Talmud and there would have been no pleasure [among the Jews] if he had shot a bullet through the window because the Jew did not want to admit that he knew about the commandment, "It is good to kill gentiles."

p. 31

We had to suffer from a fiendish German for several days. He would come and pry open all of our windows every morning at four – he explained why he did it to the soldier guards, "In order that the dogs would not be able to sleep." After prying open the windows, he took a long piece of wood and pushed everyone off the table on which they slept.

However, while we Jews had to suffer both as pawns and as Jews, our Polish co-arrestees suffered only as pawns. When the same soldiers went from our windows satisfied with teasing us, coming to the Poles' two windows, there wanting also to carry on in the same way, they had three words: "We are Aryans." That was enough for them to be left to rest.

Once we carried on a conversation with the watchmen, asking why they permitted the soldiers to come to our windows to cause trouble for us. We received an answer: "Your trouble does not interest us if a German has pleasure from it."

The German sadism was carried out against us in a sophisticated manner:

Ten people came to us; they examined everyone from head to food, chose 20 of us and left with them. The soldiers at the window immediately informed us that we would not see our comrades return. They would be shot, "Because Jews are shooting at the military in the city."

We tried to convince ourselves that as always the soldiers were only teasing in order to torture us. However, when several hours passed and our comrades had not returned, the soldiers' words began to drill into our brains. A father, who was there with a son who had been taken with the group, suffered terribly. He did not take his eyes off the door; perhaps the people would still return. The brother of Doctor Wider, who was arrested with us, was taken and he, too, was in deep despair.

p. 32

We all hung around this way for the entire day, tortured and quiet as mourners. At around 11 o'clock at night, we first heard a noise from afar and our hearts began to beat hard. We then immediately heard steps in our corridor and finally the door opened and our comrades entered. The father was beside himself with joy; the same for the doctor whose brother had returned and we all breathed easier.

Our comrades immediately began to tell us what had happened to them:

In the morning when they were taken away from us they were led into a stall where each one received a shovel with which to dig. Then they were led through the city to the Christian cemetery. There they were placed in a row and ordered to dig a large grave. This led them to suspect that they might be digging a grave for themselves. The soldiers stood over them and pressed them to work fast. The Polish overseer constantly measured if the grave was deep enough. When the work was finished, they were arranged in a row at the edge of the grave. Several were brought together and they began to beg the Germans that their lives should be spared. The soldiers ordered them to be quiet and to stand straight. They stood this way for a time that seemed like an eternity; meanwhile, again the soldiers stood themselves near them and tested their weapons, from time to time, shooting into the air. Then, our comrades were told that they would be shot in this way if something bad happened to the Germans in the city.

The Ruined Czenstochower Shul (Synagogue)
Artwork by Prof. Wilenberg

Fragment of the front wall

Murals in the synagogue

p. 33

Chapter VI

"Aryan"

A new day came again; a more beautiful, lighter sky greeted us. When we were led out of our prison room at 8 o'clock in the morning in order to have breakfast, which was brought to us by our wives, we learned the news of the city. A Jewish representative body was created among us with a chairman who was named Alibis Kapinski. This was called "Elder's Council" or *Judenrat* and its assignment was to relay all of the orders of the German regime to the Jewish population and to see to it that the orders were precisely carried out. In addition, the *Judenrat* received the assignment of taking money from the rich Jews and creating a kitchen and a hospital for the poor.

In the afternoon, we were again suddenly led out onto the tennis court. We were allowed to stand in uncertainty for a long time until several officers came over to us and ordered us to stand in rows. An old military man erected a photographic apparatus and took a photograph. Afterwards, he asked each one about his occupation. The old officer approached us humanly and this made us a little bolder and we clarified for him that we were here by chance and we asked him to release us. The officer, first of all, countered with a lecture about the war:

– Who is responsible for the war? – he said and immediately answered himself that the English were responsible. The Poles, he said, would never have dared to carry out a war against Germany. However, he said further, our military is already standing at the gates of Warsaw and the war will soon be over.

p. 34

Switching then to our matter, he told us that he had come from the city of Radomsko. Hostages were also taken there, but there they were changed every three days because the same people did not need to constantly suffer for the entire city.

Later we learned that he was the commandant of the city military garrison and, also, that the city was under his command. We decided to write a request that a delegation of our wives would bring to him. We wrote the request in the name of all of the hostages – Jews and Christians. However, when we turned to the Christians for a signature, they said to us that they had already written a request on their side because, "In today's times, "Aryans" do not need to submit any requests with Jews." We, therefore, signed the request alone, which was delivered to the commandant's adjutant the next morning.

When we gathered to go out onto the court as usual on another day, the soldiers ordered us to take all of our things with us because we would be freed.

We were astonished and quickly were ready to go out and we immediately stood in the military manner – three to a row.

We were again on the familiar tennis court. We did not want to take the food that our wives had brought because we would soon be back home. The time that the wives were permitted to remain with us passed and they had to leave us. They would wait for us by the gate of the barracks. After a long wait, the barracks commandant came and ordered us to assemble for going home. We all stood ready; he turned to us and said that he had received a decree to free the hostages - however, only the "Aryans." The Jews were to remain in the barracks as hostages.

p. 35

The "Aryans" left. Several of them, with whom we were acquainted, told us secretly, that a delegation with Bishop Brasz had made an effort for them. They promised to make an effort for us if it was possible.

We slowly went back, sad and dejected, to our prison room and again began sitting. Who knew for how long? We again began thinking of our situation; how could we understand this? In a city of 120,000 people, 95,000 "Aryans" and 25,000 Jews, we, only 35 Jews, were hostages? That is, to be responsible with our lives that no one in the entire population would do injury to a German? Could we keep the entire population loyal to we 35 Jews?

Meanwhile, day after day passed. They had started to bring groups of captive Polish military each day. We heard that the Germans had occupied large areas of our country. It became quiet in the city and we decided that our wives should again turn to the old garrison commandant with a plea for our release.

In about several days, we were ordered to gather our things and leave the barracks. The barracks commandant told us that we remained hostages of the city, but that we would be at our homes. After 27 days, we were finally freed from arrest in the barracks. However, we continued to carry the responsibility for the calm of the city.

Chapter VII

The First Edicts

An oppressive mood held sway in the city. Soldiers stood watch in front of the most beautiful buildings. The Germans had set up their offices there. The residents of these houses were simply driven out of their apartments.

The streets were full of the military; large flags with swastikas fluttered everywhere; airplanes flew, motorcycles and autos drove quickly through the streets; the windowpanes were pasted paper strips. There were few civilians and those that did appear, ran quickly through the street wanting to return more quickly to their houses.

In the morning after my liberation, when I intended to go out into the city, I was stopped at the gate by an unknown woman. She told me that the Germans were grabbing Jews for work and, in addition, they were beating them. Every German was able to have Jews at his disposal, as it pleased him. When Germans got out of the train, they stopped passers-by on the street and asked, "*Jude* [Jew]?" They made a point of seeking out the better dressed and then ordered them to carry their packages. The Jews had to bring order to the houses into which the Germans moved. Jewish women – and a point was made of choosing the rich and intelligent – had to clean the windows, doors and floors, clean the stairs, wash the toilets, cook and do all of the dirty work. While working, they were bothered by the soldiers and insulted with the dirtiest expressions.

Poland was divided; Russia occupied the eastern realms and the Germans annexed a large part of the western realms to their country, so that the Polish land that had numbered 35 million people was reduced to a population of 20 million. This country then received the name "General Government" and a government was appointed with Governor Doctor Hans Frank as the head. The capital city was Krakow and Dr. Frank and his government settled there.

The General Governor Frank issued a decree that each Jew, male and female, from age 12 on take steps to wear a white band on the right arm on which a Jewish star had to be sewn. The band had to be 10 centimeters wide. Converts were also counted as Jews. "Aryans," who had a Jew in their family up to three generations back, also had to wear the bands. All Jewish businesses, factories, artisan shops and all firms that operated even with only a portion of Jewish capital, had to hang out large boards with blue Jewish stars in the windows, entrance doors and, also, inside. Doctors, too, had to paint Jewish stars on their signs. The law went into effect on the 27th of December 1939.

The *Judenrat* had to make sure that the bands would be finished on time. And suddenly, on a beautiful morning, they appeared on all the streets. Jews felt dispirited, particularly in meeting with "Aryans": for the Germans, this was handy – they no longer needed to bother asking the passersby: "*Jude?*" They seized a person with a white band for work and treated him like a slave.

Jews were punished for not wearing the white band. The first time, a Jew had to go to the police or be imprisoned. There he was reminded of his childhood: lowered his breeches and was given a whipping of 20 lashes, and after promising that he would never again forget the band, he was released. Several weeks later the penalty became harsher – six months imprisonment and still later, if one met a Jew without a band, he could be shot on the spot.

p. 38

In the same month the General Government issued another order that no Jew could leave his residence, could not travel by train without special permission from the regime. Jews stopped wandering from our city.

Products and goods were more expensive each time, because Jewish businesses had to send "Aryans" to take care of business matters. Several took the money and the goods.

And the local regime issued anti-Jew edicts: while the non-Jewish population could move in the city from 5 in the morning until 11 at night, the Jews could only be in the street from 6 to 8 in the evening. Several minutes later, autos appeared in the Jewish streets with gendarmes who seized "tardy" Jews. They also barged into the courtyards where Jews lived, and if they did not encounter any Jews, they dragged them out of the residences and filled the cars, in order to show their elders that they were working industriously. The Jews were taken to the political commissariat where each had to pay 100 *zlotys* as a fine and 20 *zlotys* for the trip in the auto. In addition, it was necessary to sit the entire night in a cellar. Whoever had no money had to remain until someone came to ransom him.

The German commandants of the city turned over the regime to a civilian city managing committee. Dr. Richard Wendler, the police general, was chosen as the city chief. [Translator's note: Yad Vashem describes Dr. Richard Wendler as an *SS-Brigadefuehrer*, brigade leader.]

The city chief gave the *Judenrat* control over all of the Jews in our city. The first requirement from the Jews was a contribution of 400,000 *zlotys*. The *Juden- rat* succeeded in carrying out the first order, sending challenges to the well-to-do Jews that they deliver a specific sum to the treasury of the council and when the assembled sum was not sufficient, money was again demanded, until the contribution was paid.

p. 39

The *Judenrat* became a power that was able to have at its disposal the possessions of every Jew, such as the furniture, linen, dwellings and even the Jew himself, sending them to work wherever the German regime indicated. The *Judenrat* grew into a large administrative operation with various divisions. Lawyers, doctors, intelligentsia and half-intelligentsia and ordinary Jews made an effort to obtain a position in the *Judenrat* without a salary, because a *Judenrat* position was more secure than to be on the street when Jews were being seized for work. The German regime was established by Hitler's regime throughout the entire General Government, in all of the cities and *shtetlekh*, in order to make it easier for the Germans to obtain all of the Jewish possessions, starting with furniture and then gold and diamonds, businesses, factories, workshops, with the entire life and soul of the Jews.

Chapter VIII

Vandalism by the "*Folks-Deutschn*"

As soon as the Germans appeared to occupy every area of Poland, a special category of people immediately grew out of the ground that were designated by the name *folks-deutschen* [Polish-born Germans]. It was thus with us in our city. The local population knew the freshly baked "*Folks-Deutschen*" very well; they were always Poles. However, after the arrival of the Germans, these Poles began to wear special badges by which they were now transformed into "Germans."

p. 40

As it was later learned, they were German spies who occupied Polish state offices before the war. Some really were distantly descended from Germans and even had German names.

These *Folks-Deutsch* made sure that when the Poles left the city, nothing was disturbed. Then they helped the Germans settle down and revealed where everything was hidden.

The first public anti-Jewish appearance on the part of the *Folks-Deutschen* in our city was the destruction of the Jewish synagogues. They organized the Polish anti-Semites, who they knew well from before the war, for this purpose. And on a November day in 1939 with a horde of street-youths, they entered the city synagogue and there created a ruin: tearing out the doors, breaking the windows, chopping up the *ahron kodesh* [ark containing the Torah scrolls], tearing down the balconies of the women's gallery. Dozens of gentiles carried pieces of wood from the broken chairs and tables until the synagogue was empty, with peeled naked walls.

The *beis-medrash* [house of study] that had been built several years before and named for the deceased local rabbi, Reb Nukhem Asz, of blessed memory, had the same fate.

These actions of vandalism crushed the mood of the entire Jewish population. Not only the religious, but also the non-religious felt offended and insulted. It made a strong impression on a portion of the Poles, too. However, the greatest part of the Polish population joked and looked at the ruins with satisfaction.

On the 25th of December 1939, on the night of the Christian holiday, the large synagogue was set on fire; it had been considered one of the most beautiful buildings in our city. It had a beautiful, wide entrance, long stairs, and high spacious rooms. The beautiful synagogue burned the entire night and for days after, people came to quiet Wilson Street to look at the heroic action of the Germans.

p. 41

While the Polish underworld plundered the destroyed synagogues and carried out everything possible, the Germans filmed these scenes. Later, these pictures were shown in movie theaters with inscriptions about how the Poles were taking revenge against the Jews.

The Germans also claimed their share of the spoils from the burned synagogue. They had complete control over those things of value that remained. The ironwork in the walls, the metal parts at the entrance, stairs and fencing – all of this was torn out of the walls and the impact on the Jewish population was as if pieces were being ripped from a living body.

Chapter IX

Taxes and Evictions

The German administration apparatus worked fast. The various offices were established quickly, among them the tax office. Everyone immediately received orders to pay all pre-war taxes. As no one wanted to come into conflict with the German regime, each Jew paid that which was demanded of him.

By chance, the German finance inspector was a considerate person and he took it upon himself that all of the taxes from years ago did not have to paid all at once, nor those which had been cancelled long ago by the Polish tax office. If someone turned to him with a plea, he provided relief in paying out the proposed tax debt. However, there were Polish clerks from before who remained in the tax office. They "clarified" for the inspector that the Jews were rich and that if it was required, they would pay. A Jewish woman was unable to pay the taxes and cried before the German inspector. The Polish clerks laughed and said to the German that Jews do not cry with tears but with water. They belittled the Jews in the eyes of the not yet corrupted German inspector. These clerks also had a hand in general in looking up old, long cancelled tax debts. So in addition to the Germans, we also had local enemies who made every step of our lives difficult.

p. 42

The Germans felt as if they were at home in our city and began to bring people from Germany to settle here. German clerks with their wives and children came and it was necessary to arrange for apartments, furniture, linen, bedding and endless things. This would be taken care of very quickly in this way: very early, when the day was just beginning and people were still asleep, the German gendarmes surrounded a house, several houses or an entire street of houses. At the same time other gendarmes entered the residences and ordered the Jews to leave the house in the course of 10 minutes. Everyone was permitted to take only a small pack with the most necessary things and had to wait in the courtyard until the pack was searched. Half of the packs were taken in the courtyard and after receiving a few blows, the Jews were thrown out into the street.

The families who were driven out – men, women, children and the old, who only a half an hour earlier were found in a well-established home, went out to the street slowly, homeless and robbed of their most necessary things; they went crying to their closest ones or to acquaintances, who would perhaps suffer the same fate tomorrow.

p. 43

Being driven from one's home caused a panic. Jews sought advice on how to prevent becoming completely destitute in the course of several minutes. People sought out Polish acquaintances and asked them to take the furniture, furs, clothing, linens and all of their best things so that they did not fall into the hands of the Germans. The Poles did the favor for their Jewish acquaintances and took the things until the bad times for their good Jewish friends would pass. Some Jews again sold their best things to the Poles very cheaply to prevent seeing their greatest enemy robbing it all.

In addition to residences for the clerks, the Germans also needed large and beautiful meeting rooms for their offices. One day the *Judenrat* received an order to send workers with horses and wagons to the Jewish *gymnazie* [high school]. Germans already lived there who ordered the Jews to take away everything that was in the building to the German warehouse where the things that were looted from the Jews were assembled. The *gymnazie* building was taken over for the organization of labor offices. The Jewish workers immediately drove the wagons loaded with school benches, tables, armoires, teacher's lecterns and other furniture through the streets. Again, another Jewish building became a ruin.

On another day, an order came from the person in command of the city; the Jewish *gymnazie* building was to be remodeled. Jewish engineers from the technical division of the *Judenrat* immediately began the work of restoring the building with Jewish workers and tradesmen. Day after day, the Jewish workers worked at the German Pitom and Raamses [Translator's note: ancient Egyptian cities cited in the Book of Exodus, chapter 1:11] and by night they were seen coming back exhausted with their tools in their hands, head bent down to the earth, the white bands of shame on their arms, embittered that they were succeeding with their own hands, with Jewish hands, at ruining the Jewish cultural position and making preparations for the greatest enemy of the Jews.

p. 44

On a certain day the telephone rang at the *Judenrat*; it was a representative of the person in command of the city and he ordered Kapinski, the chairman of the *Judenrat*, to report to him immediately. The chairman went away very quickly to the city chief and immediately came back dejected. He immediately called a session for the *Judenrat* and reported that he had received an order from the city headquarters that all of the Jewish hospital buildings be made ready, all of the things removed and the building turned over to the gendarmerie. This had to be done quickly because the order was submitted with a short deadline.

Very early in the morning we could see Jewish tenants were being thrown out of a house. Jewish workers, under the order of the German gendarmes, were taking away the furniture from there to the German warehouses.

Now the Jewish hospital had to move into a house.

The Jewish hospital was located beyond the bridge, near the shore of the Varta. It consisted of 10 very beautiful buildings. White beds for the Jewish sick stood in clean rooms with white glossy walls. A kitchen, laundry, offices and dwelling for doctors and clerks were arranged in other buildings. A large garden with benches was located around the buildings.

The Jewish population of our city built and supported the hospital for dozens of years. Rich Jews gave large sums of money and all of the Jews paid a monthly tax for the hospital. Czentochower Jews were proud of their hospital. And the entire hospital had to be moved into several dirty rooms somewhere on a back street. Everything had to be done very quickly so that there was no time to look around at what happened here. Painters were already going with their ladders in order to whiten with lime several rooms there, from which the Jewish inhabitants had been thrown out the night before. It was necessary to organize a small hospital quickly. Thin Jewish horses with broken wagons brought the beds, the tables, chairs and other equipment from the Jewish hospital. Meanwhile, everything was thrown into the small courtyard until the rooms were limed.

p. 45

The day was dreary. A thin spray of rain fell from the sky and settled like drops of sweat on the white hospital beds, on the thin horses, on the remaining hospital equipment that lay around on the dirty courtyard and on the doctors who came here to take a look at how the hospital would look in this new place.

The work was done quickly; everyone hurried in order to keep to the deadline, which the person in command of the city had given for the move.

The fresh lime on the walls still was not dry and beds, tables and all of the other things were thrown into the rooms.

On a certain day the very ill were brought over and those who still could stand up alone were discharged from the hospital.

Thus did the Germans rob the Jewish population of its hospital building.

✳   ✳
✳

The German occupation regime also did not forget to provide for the military, even houses of prostitution. And salons had to be supplied for this purpose.

This fate also fell upon the only Jewish hotel in the city, Hotel Kupjecki at *Aleja* no. 18.

In the middle of a clear day, the German gendarmes attacked this Jewish hotel, threw out the old owner and his family. They were badly beaten and the women were brought in for prostitution.

A watchman, who controlled the entry cards to the women, was placed in front of the gate.

This "prostitution house" was "active" day and night and the surrounding neighbors did not have any rest from the constant adventures and scandals that were constantly played out.

After a time, the space proved to be too small and the regime found another Jewish house for this purpose:

In addition to the Jewish *gymnazie*, there was another middle school for Jews in our city that was the property of Dr. Akser. He constructed the building with his own money and was also the director of the school. This school was located near the main post office on a quiet street.

The German regime chose this building for the military "prostitution house." On a certain day, Dr. Akser and his wife were thrown out of their residence and from the entire building. They were forbidden to take even the least trifle with them; they even had to leave their personal underwear. The school furniture and all of the things in their residence had to be taken by Jews to the German warehouses and when all of the rooms were emptied, the *Judenrat* received an order to equip the house with luxury, so that the military men would have all of the comforts with which to enjoy themselves.

The *Judenrat* provided the needed workers and materials and large parlors, corridors and rooms were created in the house.

p. 47

The *Judenrat* confiscated the most beautiful furniture that could be found from the richest Jews for the military "prostitution house." The floors were covered with Persian rugs. The walls were adorned with Kilim rugs and expensive pictures; the parlors and rooms were lit with the most beautiful lamps and chandeliers that it was possible to obtain. Luxurious sofas, beds, blankets, bedding and everything needed in such a "recreational premises" were provided.

Dozens of the best Jewish tradesmen were employed in this work for many weeks.

The representative of the city chief would often visit the house as it was being renovated. He would always take a "riding crop" with him with which he beat the Jewish workers, hurrying them in their work.

When the facility was arranged, the *Judenrat* received an order to provide the most expensive satin lingerie for the women. And when finally everything was ready, the representative of the city chief with his "riding crop" in his hand gave an order: "*Yuden, macht dos eir wegkomt!*" [Jews, work, before you disappear!] From that day on, no Jew was permitted to appear at the house.

Chapter X

In the Clutches of the Gestapo

A long red flag with a large swastika fluttered over a beautiful new house on Kilinksi number 10. The flag was so big that it gave the impression that it would cover the entire three-story building.

This was the office of the Gestapo.

p. 48

We had heard even before the war what the Gestapo was: the Gestapo members beat and murdered their political opponents, tortured them in concentration camps; they were deadly and the marking on their uniforms was a skull. Each of them was a *malekh-hamoves* [angel of death].

However, here we could see close-up and feel on our own bodies what the Gestapo was:

Once at midday on a *Shabbos*, when a number of Jews were on the street in their best clothing, the Gestapo started to chase the young and old women. They gathered a large group and led them to the city hall square where building material lay – bricks, stones, lime and other things. Here the women were ordered to take off their winter coats or furs, lay them on the side of the open square and to start to work, which consisted of carrying the bricks and stones from one end of the square and then back to the same spot from which they were taken.

The Christian passers-by, who stopped to watch the spectacle, made fun of and laughed at the women, who were being tormented and insulted in such a brutal way. The torture stopped only when it became dark. Not all of the women found their coats; many coats were stolen by the crowd. The Germans stood in two rows at the exit of the square and permitted the women to go by, hitting them with riding crops. The Polish crowd laughed with pleasure and accompanied the beaten women with insults and curses. The Jewish women felt the taste of belittlement not only by the Germans, but also by their local Polish fellow citizens.

A similar thuggish action during the same winter month at the end of 1939 was carried out by the gendarmerie officer Ambros with his comrades:

AUFRUF
an die jüdische Bevölkerung.

Auf Grund des § 3 der zweiten Durchführungsvorschrift zur Verordnung vom 26. Oktober 1939 über die Einführung des Arbeitszwanges für die jüdische Bevölkerung des Generalgouvernements (Verordnungsblatt G. G. P. Seite 246) verfüge Ich:

Die arbeitszwangspflichtigen männlichen Juden, wie auch die getauften Juden, in Tschenstochau der Geburtsjahrgänge 1914 bis inklusive 1923 melden sich beim Ältestenrat in Tschenstochau, Marienallee № 9, während der Amtsstunden 9-15 Uhr zwecks Eintragung in die Arbeitszwangskartei in der Reihenfolge:

am 9. März 1940 mit den Anfangsbuchstaben A-H

am 10. März 1940 mit den Anfangsbuchstaben I-R

am 11. März 1940 mit den Anfangsbuchstaben S-Z

Die Nichtbefolgung dieser Anordnung wird mit Zuchthaus bis zu 10 Jahren bestraft. Daneben kann auf Einziehung des gesamten Vermögens erkannt werden.

Tschenstochau, den 8. März 1940

Der Stadthauptmann
(-) Dr. WENDLER.

WEZWANIE
do ludności żydowskiej.

Na podstawie § 3 drugich przepisów wykonawczych do rozporządzenia Generalnego Gubernatorstwa z dnia 26. października 1939 r. w sprawie wprowadzenia przymusu pracy dla ludności żydowskiej (Dziennik Rozporządzeń Generalnego Gubernatora Str. 246) zarządzam:

Podlegający obowiązkowi pracy przymusowej mężczyźni Żydzi w Częstochowie oraz Żydzi ochrzczeni roczników 1914 do 1923 r. włącznie winni się zameldować w Radzie Starszych w Częstochowie przy ul. N. P. Marii № 9, celem zarejestrowania się w kartotece pracy przymusowej w godzinach między 9-15 w następującym porządku:

w dn. 9. marca 1940 z nazwiskami rozpoczynającymi się od A-H

w dn. 10. marca 1940 z nazwiskami rozpoczynającymi się od I-R

w dn. 11. marca 1940 z nazwiskami rozpoczynającymi się od S-Z

Niewykonanie niniejszego zarządzenia podlega karze w domu pracy przymusowej, do lat 10. Niezależnie od tego może być orzeczona konfiskata całego majątku.

Częstochowa, dnia 8. marca 1940 r.

Starosta Grodzki
(-) Dr. WENDLER.

Notices about Forced Labor for Jews

p. 49

Once at 12 midnight, they surrounded several Jewish streets and ordered all of the Jews to come out to the new market, threatening to shoot those who remained in their residences. Everyone came out and stood in the middle of the snow, in freezing weather and strong winds. The tortured stood this way until 5 o'clock. Then the hooligans led them to their barracks. There they were ordered to get completely undressed, naked. The gendarmes searched through the clothing, took money, watches, rings and everything that had any form of worth. The naked women were thrown on the tables by the gendarmes for a thorough examination. The torture lasted until 6 o'clock in the evening. Then the women were thrown out of there insulted, morally and physically broken, half dressed.

The suffering Jews and their wives went to the *Judenrat* to complain about the gendamerie. However, the *Judenrat* could not help in any way. The *Judenrat* only had the right to do with their Jews whatever was necessary so that the orders from the regime were quickly and exactly carried out. It had no right whatsoever to intervene about injustices the Germans did to the Jews.

*　*
*

On a cloudy afternoon, the Gestapo drove in autos to Garibaldi Street to a certain Jew name Lenczner. Lenczner was not then at home and the Gestapo first demanded that Lenczner's wife give them a stick. As there were no sticks to be found in the house, the woman had to get one from a neighbor. Meanwhile, Lenczner arrived and the Gestapo took him and his wife into a room from which a neighbor immediately heard blows and screams through the wall. The German hit Lenczner on his head with the stick that his wife had brought and shouted, "Give us money, gold, diamonds!" The couple opened a cabinet, took out the jewelry and all of the valuable items and gave them to the thugs. However, this was not enough for them and they pointed their revolvers at Lenczner and ordered him to turn towards the wall. His wife then fell to their feet and begged them to allow her husband to live. They then ordered the man to undress completely and to lie on the table. They again began to beat him murderously and when he bent from pain, they forced his wife to hold her husband's feet so that they would not move. The couple cried terribly and screamed and their cries carried to the street. However, the murderers so lost control that the more their victims cried and screamed, the more severe were the blows with the stick over the Jew's naked body. Lenczner's children cried terribly in the kitchen and tore their clothing from their bodies in grief. In the end, the Jew fainted and his wife poured water over him in order to revive him. When the murderers saw that he no longer was moving, they hit him still more, until his body became black.

p. 50

Before they left, they hit the wife a few times and told her that they should come to the Gestapo tomorrow at four in the afternoon and bring all the valuable items.

When the Gestapo bandits left, the neighbors began to revive the Jew. A doctor was called who gave him injections and said that he should be wrapped in wet sheets. When he began to regain consciousness, they became concerned as to how to make it possible for him to go to the Gestapo office tomorrow, as the murderers had warned before leaving.

p. 51

Lenczer's family members went to the *Judenrat* and explained what happened to them. The chairman of the *Judenrat* just helplessly raised his shoulders. What could he do against the Gestapo? They went to a Jew named Wajnrib, who had certain acquaintances in the Gestapo and could sometimes have edicts revoked with the payment of a sum of money.

However, Wajnrib, too, only shook his head in this case: he didn't know if he would have the opportunity to speak with the same Gestapo members who had been at the Lenczners. However, he would try to do something, if it was possible.

In the morning when the designated hour neared, the severely ill Lenczner got out of bed with great effort. His wife and children dressed him, took him down the stairs and put him in the horse cab – he could not sit. His daughter held him so that he would not fall and thus they went to the Gestapo office, bringing their family jewelry and money.

Lenczner, with his damaged body, barely made it up to the second floor of the Gestapo house. He was taken into a room in which the people who had beaten him the day before were sitting. One of them asked him:

– Have you pulled out the gold from the holes? And who is she?" – He pointed to the woman who had accompanied Lenczner.

– This is my father – the daughter answered – he cannot go alone, so I helped him come here.

They laid out the things brought with them. The two murderers looked at everything precisely, took the golden objects, diamond rings and the money; recognizing the silver candlesticks with the menorah they returned them. One of the two wrote an enumerated list, which he laid on the table and said: "Sign it!" Lenczner signed immediately, not looking at what was on the list. The enumerated list was read aloud and it stated that during the search of the residence of the Jew Lenczner, 1,000 *zlotys* were found that were requisitioned for the benefit of the German Reich according to the "law" that a Jew may not have more than 200 *zlotys* in cash.

p. 52

Lenczner left for home with this list, pleased that it had ended "well" and he spent a month in bed while the wounds on his body healed.

✳ ✳
✳

The leader of the Gestapo was named Kriger. The Jews had to endure great misery from him. On the first day that he appeared, he immediately ordered that the Jewish residents should clean the houses and the streets under the supervision of the current Polish house watchmen. Every morning, he controlled the Jews at work and observed if the house watchman was paying close attention to how the Jews worked. Every day he found new ways in which to torment and belittle the Jewish residents. Once, for instance, he asked that stones be thrown from one place to another and then back. Another time he selected similar "work" and thus, each time he found new sadistic pranks. The Jewish women had to wash the communal toilets in the houses, the stairs and other dirty areas.

He ordered that the watchmen in the Jewish houses – who were all Polish – should move into the apartments of the owners and the owners into the apartments of their watchmen. In the houses of the Christian owners, he ordered a Jewish tenant to give his residence to the watchman and move into the watchman's residence. Also, private residences had to be cleaned up and purified by the Jews and the entire house, in which their residence was located. He always went around with a riding crop of twisted wire and lead, and beat every passing Jew, woman and child. He also would help the *Folks-Deutsch*, who were supported by the administrators in the Jewish houses, collect rent from the Jewish tenants. He and the *Folks-Deutsch* would go into a house and order all of the Jews to appear on a spot. When the Jews went down to the courtyard, the Gestapo person stood them in a line, casting venomous looks at them and began to beat them without distinction – men, women and children – until they were covered in blood. Then he gave them work to do: throwing stones from place to place under the supervision of the Polish watchmen.

p. 53

After two hours, when the Jews already were exhausted from the work, he again stood them in rows, again beat them on the head and spoke as follows: You dogs! The rent that you owe up to today and in addition for the coming month, you should immediately pay in advance. And from today you should bring the money in advance to the German gentleman (pointing to the _Folks-Deutsch_).

It should be understood that this money immediately went into the pocket of the administrator. For the tenant, who was unable to pay, others paid in order to get rid of these people more quickly.

Soon after we read in the German newspapers that this Kriger was chosen as Gestapo chief for the entire "General Government." Suddenly, we saw what kind of "great" man we had had here.

* *
*

p. 54

Germans and a number of _Folks-Deutsch_ occupied the leadership offices in the Gestapo. Poles were employed as secret agents.

There was one, who was a Polish policeman before the war; under the German occupation he became a _Folks-Deutsch_. He was named Szabelski. He knew the people of our city very well. Right from the start, he went after the Jews. He was the leader at all of the searches. He only spoke German and he beat Jews murderously. His greatest pleasure was to see Jewish blood. He did not leave a Jewish house until he made someone there a cripple.

* *
*

Once in the morning I went out to the street. Suddenly I felt a sturdy hand on my arm. I turned around and saw a Polish train official standing before me. He said to me:

– Where is your armband? You are obviously a Jew!

I looked at my right arm and saw that I had forgotten to put on the armband. The train official immediately told me to go the police commissariat. I told the person who led me that today I had put on different clothes and forgot to put on the armband. This did not interest him. One could not forget. In addition, he said, train officials had to carry out the orders of the Gestapo.

We arrived at the premises of the Polish police; the policeman on duty asked for my identification and after I answered him, he requested a small monetary fine from me. When I laid out the money on the table, from a second room, a taller police official appeared who was once friendly with me, and hearing what had happened, he announced tersely: "Jews who are detained without armbands need to be sent to the Gestapo." I tried to defend myself, explaining why I had been without an armband today. However, my former "friend" did not even want to listen to me politely. I was detained until the commissar came and when he came, my former "friend" tried to have me sent to the Gestapo.

p. 55

I found myself in a cell one meter wide and three meters long. There was only a long small bench and a pail. The floor was made of stone; a small barred window was on the ceiling, smeared with lime. It was terribly cold, even though it was sunny outside. The hours passed slowly in hunger and cold. Finally, I heard heavy steps. The door opened and I was given an order: "Out!" I was led into the same room in which I had been in the morning. A man in civilian clothes was there. At the same time, Wajnrib appeared. He said, pointing to me, "This is my cousin, for whom I asked today." The civilian turned to me angrily: "Why do you not want to wear the band of shame, do you want to pass as a Christian?"

I noticed my coat with the band, which I had left in my residence today, lay on a bench. I understood that my coat was brought in order to see if the band was there. I again explained that I had forgotten to put the band on my arm. The civilian took a long twisted whip out of his desk; he showed it to me and said:

– If you were not Wajnrib's cousin, you would have received 20 lashes! However, if you are caught again without an armband, I will order that a Jewish *Mogen Dovid* [Jewish star] be burned onto your forehead with a glowing piece of iron.

p. 56

Chapter XI

Persecutions and Robbery

The German regime gave out an order that all Polish officials must return to the posts they held before the occupation. The Polish officials were enlisted to return to their offices very quickly. A German was found as the manager of every office and his closest co-worker was a *Folks-Deutsch.*

The city managing committee worked under the leadership of a local well-known Polish merchant, Pawel Belka. This Belka was a German agent during the First World War and he also became one this time, as soon as the Germans entered our city.

As a merchant, he had many Jewish acquaintances, who independently now tried to ask for a favor. Belka did not refuse; however, he also did not do anything. He was not good and not bad.

A Polish newspaper quickly began to be published that printed the ugliest of defamations of Jews and attempted to prove that the former Polish government together with the Jews was guilty in the war. This work of incitement became more frequent and more venomous. And since this newspaper was the sole source of news, it had many readers. The editors did not have any difficulties finding collaborators, because there was never a lack of Polish anti-Semites here.

p. 57

Dr. Frank, too, was not lacking in venomous incitement against the Jews in an appeal by the General Government to the Polish population. The former Polish police also contributed its share to the persecutions in relation to the Jewish population. The German regime reorganized the former Polish police, leaving them in the same uniforms as before the war. The policemen received the same salaries as before; they carried out their police functions with the German gendarmes. The Polish policemen knew every person in the city and knew how they were employed. In addition, pairs were created: a German gendarme and a Polish policeman. Among other assignments, they also controlled the prices in the businesses. It should be understood that they gave their primary attention to Jewish businesses and always found some offense. The Polish policeman and the German gendarme would take part in the "work" – the policeman searched for some underground "crime" and informed the gendarme and this one beat the Jews until they were bloodied. Then, together, they took anything they wanted and divided the spoils.

*   *
*

Need continued to increase among the robbed and tortured Jewish population. Street trading arose. Children and adults as well stood in the streets and carried out a pitiful trade with goods that were held hidden in bags: soap, saccharin, thread and other small things. The policemen persecuted the small Jewish children, who were employed with this "trade," with particular savagery. The policemen would change to civilian clothes, so that they could prey upon the small "merchants." They hurled these children to the ground, beat them murderously and took their small amount of goods and money. Then the children had to go home with them to their parents where the remaining things found there were taken.

p. 58

In addition to the Polish police and the German gendarmes, the Jewish population had to endure another vicious affliction that had the name "*tzipers*." [Translator's note: a variation on the Hebrew word, *tzipor* – bird, used to describe the way the Poles who would "nip" at everything the Jews did in the manner of a bird that appropriates the food it eats.] "*Tzipers*" were Poles from various strata. They lived on what they had "nipped" from the Jews; every Jew, whatever he was employed doing, had to support several "*tzipers*" who tormented him like leeches. The "*tziper*" spied and learned where a Jew had hidden goods, then he came to the Jew and demanded money or a portion of the goods. If one refused, he brought the police who not only took the goods, but also beat and arrested the entire family.

The number of these parasites who lived at the expense of the Jews grew from day to day. They stood at the gates of the houses and watched everyone who went in and out, searched the packages that were carried in and out. They stood watch at the bakeries and food shops and other businesses and controlled everything.

And even if this were not enough, a new woe suddenly appeared. These were Polish women who established close links to the Germans. Such a woman, who had a German for a "friend," entered a Jewish business, chose the best things, and asked for the price. The merchant would give the normal price. Then the woman would leave and immediately return with a German soldier or gendarme who took the little package of goods and threw a small coin on the table, that was usually five percent of the value of the goods. The German would throw such a look at the Jews that it was enough for the Jew to know not to say a word in protest.

p. 59

The Jewish businesses would be full of such "customers." If a merchant said that he did not have the requested things and the German with the friend found them, this merchant was not someone to envy.

Chapter XII

A Message From Lodz

Suddenly new Jewish faces appeared in the streets, men and women. Closed horse cabs arrived quickly at the gates of houses, people came out who were dressed like everyone else; however, they had something on them that was new to us in Czenstochow: they wore yellow patches in the form of a *Mogen-Dovid* [Star of David], sewn on the chest and on the back. The color of the patches was such a screaming yellow that it could be recognized from a distance. We immediately learned that the Jews from the city of Lodz wore these yellow patches.

The city of Lodz did not belong to our "General Government," but to the German Reich. Now, Lodz was called "Litzmannstadt."

The Jews, who exited from the horse cabs, had barely escaped with their lives from Lodz and endured great trouble until arriving here. I started a conversation with one of the Lodzers, who told me the following history:

– There, in what was once the Polish "Manchester," a Jew does not walk in the street as you do here. You have a paradise here. There are tens of thousands of *Folks-Deutsch* in Lodz, in addition to the military and gendarmes. When a Jews appears in the street, he is beaten until bloodied. The same thing happens to the women. At every call by a German or grown German child in the street: *"Yude, Kom!"* ["Jew, come!"] – the Jews must remain standing, waiting for a blow and must do everything they are asked to do. Jews are being driven from their residences and the city is being made *"Judenrein* [cleansed of Jews]." This is being carried out quickly in this manner:

p. 60

There is in a neighborhood in Lodz with the name Balut. This was always the poorest and most neglected neighborhood in the city. The Jews received an order to move there and disappear from the remaining parts of the city. They were only permitted to take a small bundle of personal underwear. However, they had to leave their household, furniture, clothing and all of their possessions.

Thus, 100,000 Lodz Jews became poor people with one blow. We always had the richest Jews in the country in Lodz: large manufacturers who employed thousands of workers, owners of the largest wholesale businesses and manufacturing businesses in Europe, who were worth significant millions; thousands of small manufacturers of the so-called woven chairs, thousands of owners of smaller, but rich enough businesses.

At a certain moment tens of thousands of Jews – rich and poor – stood one next to the other on the Lodz Balut [market area in Lodz].

In normal times the Lodz Balut could contain 10,000 souls. Now, however, 100,000 were pressed together there. Several families lived in one room - the once rich together with the poor.

A number of Jews saved something of their personal property, selling their best things for almost nothing to their good acquaintances, "Aryans," several days before their expulsion. Others again gave to their Polish acquaintances – now *Folks-Deutschn* – their linens, furs and valuable things to be "hidden until the bad times ended" when they would take back everything.

p. 61
My new acquaintance explained further:

– Jews escaped from Lodz, if they could. There it was said that here in Czenstochow it is still bearable; I did everything in order to come here. And the truth is that compared with Lodz, it is a paradise here.

– The road from Lodz to here – he said further – is not an easy one. In my life, I traveled through dozens of borders from one country to another, but no other way was as far as the one from Lodz to Czenstochow. I traveled by train, by automobile and horse drawn cab, walked during the days. And at night, bribed Germans, *Folks-Deutschn* and Poles, gave away the most expensive things I had in my possession, until I arrived here.

– Suddenly, he said, I was a poor man. I came here to a distant relative who still considers me the earlier rich man. I am living on the last few *zlotys* that the various robbers and black mailers did not notice and take from me on the way.

Yet he appeared to be content and cried out almost with enthusiasm:

– Here I walk on the sidewalk; with us in Lodz, Jews have to walk in the street, near the gutter, where the horses go. The Jews who are caught for work here come back after several hours. On the contrary, there, if a Jew is caught for work, at best, he first returns a cripple after several days or, in general, we never see him again.

– A Pole was employed as a master craftsman in my factory, who is now a *Folks-Deutsch*. He worked for me for 25 years and lived well from his earnings from me. This *Folks-Deutsch* led me out one night from Lodz. When he went with me to the train and traveled with me as far as Koluszki, he kept bleeding me for money. In addition, he introduced several of his acquaintances who blackmailed me. They threatened me – "You are a Jew; we will summon the gendarmes here immediately." And they drew money, gold and diamonds from me. This gang searched and robbed my wife and me. And my master craftsman, too, was not ashamed of doing the same. It disgusted me to look at him.

p. 62

We traveled by horse drawn cab from Koluszki until Piotrokow. On the way we were attacked by scoundrels, who shouted: "Jews, give money!" They took everything they found from my wife and me. When we were midway, our blackmailer stopped and said that he was not traveling further. "You are giving everyone money," he said, "and where am I?" I am traveling with you and am taking you away from here, I do not deserve something?" I saw that from his point of view he was correct: why should he be worse than other Polish hooligans? In addition to that, if he left us here, we would be entirely lost. We were not able to walk and, in addition, who knows whom we could meet on the road. We took our wedding rings off of our hands and took out the last golden bracelet from a hiding place and gave them to the blackmailer. After riding for two kilometers, our blackmailer again stopped. What is it again? I asked him. He was feeding the horse, he said. Meanwhile, two automobiles were traveling in our direction. We hid in a hole near the road; they drove by without stopping. We begged our blackmailer to go farther. However, he did not answer. Only after we started to beg and scream that he should go farther, he answered that the entire business was not worthwhile to him. He was afraid, he said, of the Germans: if they caught him traveling with Jews, they would take his horse with the cab and because we would be shot, there would be no one to pay for the damage. Therefore, he demanded that we should pay now for everything. We again had to give him something and he finally moved from the spot. We saw dozens of Jews lying dead on the road.

p. 63

We had conflicts several times with our horse drawn cab that cost money each time. Even when we drove into the courtyard here, we were pursued by two Polish policemen to my relative's house and asked questions; where were we from and who are we. These questions also had to be answered with nice gifts.

My Lodz acquaintance expressed his satisfaction that his position enabled him to ransom himself with money from all of the robbers and he hoped to be able to live quietly here in Czenstochow.

I would not rob him right on the spot of this hope. Although I knew that he was wrong.

One thing was sure: the robbers would no longer have anything to rob from him.

Chapter XIII

Slavery

The German regime demanded from the *Judenrat* even more Jewish workers. The Jews were sent to work at the railway station, loading and unloading iron, coal, hay and other materials for the military; workers were sent to various jobs in the barracks and carrying coal to the offices and to the private residences of the Germans and, in general, wherever the Jewish labor force could be used.

The *Judenrat* itself employed several hundred men for various renovation work of the German's official and private premises, in moving Jewish furniture to German warehouses, to the German casinos and restaurants, in the Gestapo office and in private residences of various German officials and military personnel.

p. 64

The newly founded German firm, "*Waserwirtschaft* [Water Industry]," that had the assignment of regulating the shores near the Warta and Stradomka demanded more workers every day. There were already 1,200 Jews employed and they demanded more workers. In addition, the *Judenrat* received an order to provide several hundred construction workers that various military groups would receive to establish their trade schools and other accommodations; the city leadership also demanded working hands to clear away the wire fences that the Polish military had erected around the city.

We heard the same words constantly: "Work Jews, Jews work."

The *Judenrat* was forced to create a special office for labor matters and the office was given the name "Labor Office."

This office had to provide the German regime with a Jewish work force at every time and at every place.

At the same time, a decree was issued by the General Government for the entire country establishing forced labor for Jews from the age of 14 to 60.

The *Judenrat* labor office faced a very difficult assignment: 1,000 workers must work without wages for the Germans. However, where would all of the people come from to meet this obligation? The food products that the city managing committee divided among the Jewish population were too meager with which to get along and the prices of these products rose from day to day. The *Judenrat* therefore organized the matter of work in the following way:

Jews who were still in a position to pay to avoid forced labor were taxed with a fixed sum, with which those who were sent to work for the Germans without pay were supported. Thus was created two kinds of people: payers and workers. The *Judenrat* paid out small sums to the workers, gave them bread, organized kitchens where they received lunch, bought paper suits and wooden shoes for them. The charge for not having to work was small at first and in time it was raised.

p. 65

Despite all of the efforts by the *Judenrat,* the needs of the workers became even greater. The labor office, therefore, raised its charge to the non-working people, in order to have more money. However, the problem was not solved because there was constantly a rapid "transfer": yesterday's "taxpayers" became today's workers; the earnings could be seen to disappear and there remained even fewer people who could ransom themselves from work. The rows of workers, therefore, grew constantly and the rows of payers grew smaller by the day. And as there were fewer payers, the charges had to be even higher.

However, the Germans constantly kept demanding still more people for work. The labor office was, therefore, forced to call to work, those who paid the work tax. In a short time all men up to age 45 had to be called to work.

Only the very rich and people older than 45 up to age 60 who had the ability to pay could ransom themselves from work.

However, the demands of the Germans for work hands grew so that in the end the labor office had to call even those who paid great sums to the work fund. Thousands of demands were sent out each day to those who had paid requiring them to appear at the designated office for work on another day.

p. 66

Conditions became even more difficult; the slavery greater. Very often the German leaders of various workshops who did not receive the number of workers demanded by a set deadline, entered the *Judenrat* and beat the leader and the Jewish clerk and took the entire staff to work. Then the entire administration of the *Judenrat* stopped. Only when the president of the *Judenrat* provided other workers and, on several occasions intervened, were the clerks from the *Judenrat* released. It also often occurred that if the *Judenrat* did not provide the workers demanded at the set time, the German gendarmes and the Polish police went out into the city in autos and fenced off the streets, catching every Jewish passerby, taking men from their businesses and houses, leaving everything abandoned.

With shouting and a roar of wild animals, the Jews were driven to a square. Then they were sent in groups to the outskirts of the city to large wooden barracks that had been erected not long ago for who knows what purpose. The Jews were detained in these barracks; from there they were sent out to work and after work they had to return to the barracks. They were guarded by German gendarmes and Polish policemen who treated them as slaves.

When several days passed, and these people did not come home, their wives and relatives ran to the *Judenrat* asking it to intervene with the regime. It was learned that the Germans demanded a large payment for each one who would be freed. The *Judenrat* would by chance also have benefit to its treasury and count on a certain sum, in addition to what was demanded by the Germans. Those who had money ransomed themselves from the bandits and the poor or stubborn remained in the barracks for several weeks. The people became weakened by the heavy work because of bad nutrition, no opportunity to get enough sleep, with the worst hygienic conditions, and a typhus epidemic broke out. Then the Polish and German police were withdrawn from there and the *Judenrat* was given the responsibility to insure that the Jews did not leave the barracks.

p. 67

Seeing how this matter was taking on such a terrible direction, the relatives and wives of those interned in the barracks made the greatest efforts, sold everything they had left and ransomed the captives from the Germans. However, there were those who remained for whom there was no ransom money to be paid as demanded. These were taken to a new camp that had been established in a former Jewish factory, from which the Germans had taken the machines. They remained there for a long time until a sanitary commission decreed that the camp be disbanded, it should be understood, not because of the Jews, but because of the danger that illness would spread.

To the persecution and torture that the Jewish population endured from the Germans and from the Poles was added the painful feeling of being persecuted also by Jews. This was the fiendish system of the Germans that one Jew would oppress another. Jewish clerks were employed in the administration of the labor office. They sent out thousands of slips every day to the working people, gave out tickets for lunch and bread. Overseers were also employed who took the workers to their workplaces in groups. They were called "brigadiers."

p. 68

Although they themselves were workers or employees, they treated the unfortunate people who worked under their leadership very badly. There were some brigadiers who took their "office" very seriously and demanded strict obedience. If one of the workers or the entire group did not behave exactly as the brigadiers wished, they were reported to the "higher authorities." If the brigadier reported this to the Jewish labor office, they would take care of the matter among themselves as among their own. However, if the brigadier reported this to the Germans, the workers were immediately murderously beaten on the spot or they were called to the Gestapo, and it very rarely occurred that such workers would be able to return on their own strength. In the majority of the cases, such workers would have to be brought home, because they could no longer walk.

Polish brigadiers also led the Jewish labor groups. They beat the Jews as they worked. However, it was worse if they reported a transgression to the Germans. Therefore, the Jewish workers were forced to live well with their Polish brigadiers. The workers had to pay the brigadiers weekly allowances, give them food products and gifts.

Every morning at 5 o'clock there was great movement in the Jewish neighborhood and on all the large squares. The workers streamed from every house to the assembly points. Here, the brigadiers called out the names of their workers from a list and marched with them to their designated work place.

Multitudes of Jews marched. Every group was led by a brigadier. Among the thousands of the ragged and enslaved in the long rows were those who not long ago had been small and large merchants, owners of factories, professors at *gymnasium* [high school], advocates, craftsmen and workers, old and young and the very young, even children of 13. Classes or strata no longer existed – the enemy had equalized everything: Jews! Jews! Only Jews!

p. 69

At night the same multitudes came back, tired, dusty, famished. The older ones and the children could not maintain the military step that was forced on the labor groups – tired, they dragged after their group. The brigadiers hurried them along: "Faster! Join your group!"

Polish brigadiers from the firm, *Waserwirtschaft*, wanting to cheer themselves up at the expense of the Jews, would order the workers to sing on their difficult way. The content of the songs was: "The good Hitler is teaching the Jews to work." The Jews reported to the Jewish labor office every day after work with split heads and slashed bodies. However, there was no help for them there.

Chapter XIV

"Czeczanow" Labor Camp

There was a small *shtetl* in the Lublin area named Czeczanow; the Germans created a labor camp for the Jews there. The Jewish labor office received notification from the regime to provide a thousand young men from 18 to 25 years old for the Czeczanow labor camp. Clerks immediately went out with notices and demanded that the young men appear at the labor office during the course of the day in order to be sent from there to the work place.

Meanwhile, the *Judenrat* made use of the opportunity to increase its funds and permitted the rich to ransom themselves with the payment of money. It should be understood that the poor had to appear in their place.

p. 70

Several days after the young people were sent away to the camps, a letter came to us from there in which we were told that the people who had had the misfortune to be sent to this labor camp were tortured at work, murderously beaten and did not have food. The parents of the young people went to the *Judenrat* with the letter and asked for help for their children. However, just as in all other cases, the *Judenrat* could not help here.

From time to time alarming letters arrived from Czeczanow with very frightening news that the people there were being tortured to death. However, the parents of the unfortunate along with the *Judenrat* were helpless and could do nothing. Thus, the summer passed and in the autumn of 1940, escapees from the camp arrived and we learned what had happened in Czeczanow:

When the young people were sent from Czenstochow they were taken under escort by police to Lublin. There they were loaded into cattle wagons and handed over to the authority of the *S.A.* [*Sturmabteilung* – storm troopers], who especially had come from Czeczanow in order to bring the labor slaves there. When they arrived on the spot in the middle of the night, in darkness, the storm troopers drove them out of the wagons with iron whips, worse than driving cattle, and they were harassed in this way for several kilometers under lashes and blows on the way to the labor camp. When the storm troopers finally permitted the young people to catch their breath a little, they, the unfortunate, tired, fell onto the bare earth under the clear sky.

At daybreak in the morning, they were first able to see where they were. It was a wide field, in which barracks had been erected without roofs. The Jews who had been brought here earlier had prepared these.

p. 71

There was no time to look around for long because their pain began immediately.

They received their daily food portion: 100 grams of bread and a half liter of watery soup, and were compelled to work in a nearby forest where the Germans were secretly building fortifications near the then German-Russian border in the Lublin area. This was in 1940 when Germany and Russia still had a "friendly" relationship.

The Jews dug pits under the supervision of the storm troopers. Those with twisted lead riding crops sent them flying over Jewish heads during their work. The German assassins slashed at the heads of the Jewish young people, deforming faces, knocking out eyes and teeth and very often, after such an "operation" people would lie dead at the workplace. The dead were immediately thrown into the pits and covered with earth. All of the Jews were named "Israel" to them.

Jews chopped trees in the forests and the Germans beat them. There was no difference if someone worked well or not – all, without exception, were beaten severely. The assassins devised various methods of torture: suddenly the storm troopers might scream to a Jew: "*Hose runter! Arsch hoch! Lieg zich hin!*", that is, "Lower your pants, lift the lowest part of your body and lie down." Immediately, a twenty-something year old young man lay on a cut tree trunk with his naked bottom up. Two friends with whom the young man worked had to take two thin tree branches and with their entire strength beat their friend. If the assassin was not satisfied with the beating, he also ordered the two friends to lie near the first and when all three were laying, he took a piece of wood and with his entire strength began to skin and shred the flesh of their bodies until blood flowed. Often he struck long enough until the victim stopped screaming, and fainting, fell off the tree trunk onto the grass that was wet with blood. Whoever did not immediately stand up on his feet was thrown into a pit and immediately covered with dirt. It once occurred that a young man stood up in the middle of a beating and asked the storm trooper, "Why are you beating me?" This young man was punished terribly: he was forced to put his hands in his pants pockets and he was placed in a pit in this position and buried alive. Only his hair was left sticking out, so that the murderers could show what happens to those who ask questions. They said, "Jews must do everything they are ordered to do and not ask questions."

p. 72

The leader of the labor camp was a major named Dalf. In the opinion of the Jews who slaved away under his leadership, the major justly earned the title: "king of the sadists." One of his most beloved "games" was to have a row of people stand and he aimed his revolver between the eyes of his victims. However, the Jews became so indifferent to death that when the sadist initiated the "game" it no longer made any impression on them. Dying by a bullet was a "luxurious death" – it was better to be shot than to become dejected with threats or to be buried alive.

Every day Major Dalf visited the labor sites and in every division left several dead young people. Major Dalf had a son not far from the camp who would often come to visit his father. The younger Dalf enjoyed sports and particularly liked to box. He would place several Jews in a room and "teach" them to box, hitting them between the eyes, knocking out teeth and breaking noses. And when the Jews lay on the ground, he hit them over their heads with a piece of wood and chased them from there. Then he led in others in their place. The "sport" repeated itself several times in this way. The younger Dalf liked to learn how to shoot just like his father; however, not between the eyes, but in the middle of the head. He did this in this way: he ordered a Jew to run and shot after him until he had hit the middle of the head. Every time, when he came into the camp, he had to occupy himself with this kind of "sport" until he shot a bullet right in the middle of a Jew's "clever" head, as he would say.

p. 73

Major Dalf and his son had large trained dogs, which would be incited against the Jewish workers. The dogs would wildly attack the victims and tear pieces of flesh from their faces and bodies. After carrying out this bloody work, their owners would pet and caress them.

* *
*

Fresh transports of Jews from the surrounding cities and *shtetlekh* arrived every day. Old Jews also began to arrive. Certainly, there were no longer any young people in those cities. It became more crowded in the camp; masses of people were tortured and fresh ones came in their place. There were no sick people here. Everyone was healthy and strong. Every morning, when Dalf inspected his Jews and asked, who is sick, no one reported himself sick because a sick person was shot.

Once on a summer night several storm troops barged into a barrack with metal whips in their hands. The Jews who remained were laying on the bare ground. Hearing the tumult, they stood up. The storm trooper murderers, who were very drunk, ordered hundreds of Jews to line up naked in the courtyard. Several Jews were immediately shot on the spot; those remaining were ordered to march to the *shtetl*, to Czeczanow. Arriving in the *shtetl*, the people were forced to go to the cemetery naked. Only three young people succeeded in escaping along the way. When the tortured arrived at the cemetery, their bodies were skinned by the whips and burned as in a flame of fire by the blows that constantly hailed over them while being forced on their way. The assassins ordered pits to be dug, but as there were no shovels, the unfortunate ones were driven into a swamp and there they were all shot.

p. 74

Several young men in the barracks decided to escape to the Russian side. They worked diligently for several days in order not to arouse any suspicion and on a dark night they carefully left the barracks. They went into the woods and dashed for the Russian side. After several hours of losing their way, they were stopped by the Russian border guard who took them to a hearing before a military commission. They were questioned and the statements of the young men about the horrible conditions in the German labor camp were recorded. However, they were told that according to an agreement with the Germans, the Russians could not permit anyone illegal to cross the border and therefore the young men had to be sent back to the Germans. Crying or begging did not help and on a dark night, they were taken back to the border by Russian soldiers.

The desperate young men had to enter the camp covertly; there they stood with another labor group and thus erased their footprints.

The parents of the young men who labored in Czeczanow learned that their children were going around in ragged clothing. They made efforts through the *Judenrat* to receive permission to send packages of needed things. This time the regime showed "understanding" and gave permission. However, half of the things sent were immediately taken away on the spot; the storm troopers in the camp took their portion of the leftovers and the remnants reached the camp workers.

With the arrival of winter, the work of digging pits in the field stopped. For large sums of money, the storm troopers looked away when a Jew sneaked out of the camp. Several saved themselves in that way. However, the camp continued to exist and large number of Jews remained there.

Chapter XV

The Activity of the *Judenrat*

The *Judenrat* received an order from the chief of the city that the Jews should not appear too often in the streets, particularly on the main streets. There was a warning that if the "drifting about" of the Jews did not stop, the regime would bring forth "the appropriate consequences." The *Judenrat* was therefore confronted with creating a Jewish "*ordnungdinst*" [Translator's note: keepers of order, i.e. police] that would assure that the Jews would not appear in the streets too often.

Several dozen young men were recruited for the police, who were placed at watch posts along every street. These Jewish order keepers wore armbands on both arms: on the right, a white band with a *Mogen Dovid* [Jewish star] and on the left – a blue band with an inscription in German: *Judische ordnungdisnt* [Jewish police].

p. 76

Keeping order in the *Judenrat* and labor offices, in the kitchens and. in general, "disciplining" the Jewish population, also belonged to the functions of the police. The Jewish "order keepers" would immediately appear anywhere that several Jews stood together and order them to disperse.

It is understood that the authority of the Jewish police extended only to the Jews. However, they were powerless and helpless with not only those who were non-Jews, but also even with small children, if they were not Jewish.

Still more German families arrived in our city, and schools were created for their children. These school children from ages eight to 14, going to or in school would attack Jewish children and even adults and they would beat them with sticks or riding crops. When the German children were driven away by the Jews, they looked for the gendarmes, who defended the German children who had endured the injustice from the Jews and taught respect to both the Jewish children and adults, bringing their heavy hands against Jewish faces. The impudence of the little Germans therefore grew and Jews were forced to hide when they saw them in the street.

It once occurred that the leaders of the *Judenrat* and the leaders of the police were in the street when the Jewish children were beaten by the little German hooligans. The Jewish "representatives of the regime" at first tried to restrain the little Germans with moral arguments, such as "love thy neighbor,'" etc. However, the small hooligans were unimpressed by this kind of Jewish "preaching" and again did their work. Then the leader of the "Jewish police" brought his men with the armbands on both arms and tried to make order. However, the small Germans also attacked them, so that in the end a German gendarme in the street was asked to intervene. The gendarmc gave an entire sermon to the leaders of the *Judenrat* and the police that they and the uneducated Jewish children and the entire *verdammt gesellschaft* [damned society] should not disturb the tranquility of the well-educated German children. He finally told them: "You have only to order your Jews to have respect for the German children!"

p. 77

Our leaders and the police were booed by the "well educated" German children and they left in disgrace.

* *
*

The *Judenrat* received an order from the regime to register Jewish possessions on special forms that had to be filled out and given to the city chief. Every Jewish man and every Jewish woman had to provide a list of their exact possessions. The following columns were enumerated on the form: factories, businesses, workshops, securities, furniture, linen, blankets, rugs, pictures, journals and all other house wares, apparel, suits, coats, furs, shoes, hats and all other clothing (here the color of everything had to be given), gold, silver and other precious metals in every shape and form and all other things of value. Everything had to be written in the proper columns of the form and signed by the appropriate person. At the later inspections, the items found were compared with that which had been recorded on the forms. If things were found that were not recorded on the forms, they were taken and their owner was "paid" for this so that he would remember it for his entire life.

p. 78

A registration of those who wanted to go to Russia was carried out at the same time. Those people who had relatives in the cities that had been occupied by the Russians at the start of the war reported for the registration. They now imagined that they would be able to join their families. The young people also appeared for the registration. All of the registration papers were submitted by the *Judenrat* to the regime.

* *
*

Jews driven out of the surrounding *shtetlekh* by the Germans began arriving in our city. The first homeless came from the *shtetl*, Bojanow. They told of gendarmes entering the *shtetl* once in the middle of the night and everyone was driven out on the road outside the *shtetl*. They wandered in the dark until they arrived here. They first went to the *Judenrat* and settled in the courtyard, corridors, on stairs and wherever there was an empty spot – men, women, children and old people, all fatigued, tired, haggard, hungry, with dejected faces and ragged.

When night fell and the tired homeless still did not have a roof over their heads, they were quickly divided among the Jewish houses that were already too crowded because local Jews who had been thrown out by the Germans from their dwellings also had to be housed with other families.

p. 79

The next morning the *Judenrat* immediately proceeded to create shelters for the homeless. All of the premises in which *minyonim* [groups of at least ten men who pray together], *Talmud Torahs* [elementary schools for poor boys], small synagogues located deep in the courtyards were taken over for this purpose. The new synagogue that had been damaged was repaired a little to arrange for the accommodation of the homeless there.

However, the shelters quickly became overfilled. Almost everyday new people who had been driven out of their homes arrived. Our city, which had 25,000 souls before the war, grew to 40,000.

Life in the shelters became even more difficult. Men and women and their children had to live together in one room. So did people from various classes. There was a lack of beds and many had to sleep on the ground. Almost everyone was isolated and disconnected; we collected as much furniture and linens as was possible and made every effort to help out those more unfortunate than we were.

The kitchen for the homeless was constantly active. However, there was not enough food. Large kettles of food began to be cooked in private houses and brought to the kitchen. But each day the conditions for the permanent residents became worse; everyone was occupied with himself and his own family. The private help became inadequate and things became worse for the people in the shelters. Contagious diseases, such as spotted and stomach typhus, began to appear in the shelters and the houses of the poor. Disinfection vehicles drove through the poor Jewish neighborhoods and cleaned the houses. The regime ordered the *Judenrat* to provide "delousing institutions" with a quarantine facility for those covered with typhus and also to create a hospital for epidemic disease.

p. 80

Jewish doctors threw themselves into the work of fighting the contagious diseases. The former captain in the Polish army, Dr. Walberg, was given the assignment of transforming the *mikvah* [ritual bath] into a quarantine facility with delousing capabilities. A short time later the facilities opened with a room for medics, *feldshers* [health practitioners], and were helpful. A hospital for epidemic disease was created in the premises of the I.L. Peretz Jewish children's home under the direction of Dr. Kagan.

All of the residents of the shelters were taken frequently to a quarantine facility. There they had their hair cut and shaved; their clothing was disinfected and they took baths.

The *Judenrat* made collections, from those who could still give, of linens, beds, bedding, and everything that the institutions and the hospital needed. Money was collected for medicines and instruments.

The hospital immediately became filled with the sick. The quarantine facility took in hundreds of people for observation. The doctors and medics worked so energetically with the help of the entire Jewish community that in time conditions came under control.

The German sanitary regime also made use of our institutions for the non-Jewish population. All beggars and the neglected in the Polish population were brought under police supervision to the Jewish sanitary facilities and were served by the Jewish personnel. Gypsies, who were strongly persecuted by the Germans, were also brought to us.

* *
*

The privation grew constantly, so that the *Judenrat* did not have the means to help the thousands of people who did not have the possibility of earning money for their needs. It, therefore, decided to create a *Judenrat* aid committee that was to generate the funds for those Jews suffering from need. The aid committee also took under its protection all of the shelters, the two hospitals, the sanitary institutions and the entire poor Jewish population.

p. 81

The committee created separate sections for medical and economic aid. A special staff secretly investigated who was in need of help. It was discovered that people who passed as rich had for long lived in want and need. Their possessions had been taken away long ago. Others lived by selling their last possessions for a few *groshns*. It also was shown that the largest segment of the population was in need of aid.

In order to fulfill their assignment, the aid committee needed to have large sums of money. The *Judenrat* could not provide this for the use of the aid committee. Therefore, it was decided to tax even more the well-to-do Jews who still ran their business and, in this way, great sums of money flowed in.

However, despite all of this, the *Judenrat* still faced more severe problems both concerning the regime and concerning the Jewish population. Thousands of Jewish families had to be supported, thousands of workers needed to be paid daily for work that they carried out for the Germans. Several hundred *Judenrat* clerks and their departments needed to be taken care of with food. In addition to this they were paid small stipends. The *Judenrat* also needed to pay for various raw materials that were used to renovate houses for the Germans; contributions very often had to be paid for someone to be ransomed from the Gestapo. Also, despite the fact that the aid committee aided the *Judenrat's* work, with all of the demands, greater sums of money were demanded to fulfill all of the obligations that the Germans placed upon the *Judenrat*.

At the meetings of the *Judenrat*, the conclusion was reached that if the condition of the Jews in our city was not as bad as in other cities, it was only thanks to the fact that everything that was requested by the Germans was provided. Consequently, everything must continue to be done in order to satisfy their demands. Therefore, a finance commission was created whose assignment was to raise more money.

The finance commission consisted of several city council members and several people who had earlier been involved with borrowing money with interest. These people were chosen as "specialists" who knew from whom and how to extract still more money.

The finance commission created a committee in every house and a managing member was appointed for every house committee who represented the house committee at the finance commission.

Every Jew who was not utterly poor was taxed with a sum of money for the main committee. Part of the money was immediately divided among the poor Jewish residents of the house and the rest went into the treasury of the *Judenrat*..

p. 82

The map of the large and small Czentochower Ghetto

The finance commission continually thought up new taxes with various names: "premises tax" because one still lived in a corner of a room and not on the street; a "tax for order keepers" because they were "teaching" how to stand at ease; a "kitchen tax" because you did not need to use the communal kitchen; "worker tax" because you worked less than others; an "electricity tax," "hospital tax," "special tax" and more and more. Craft workers who were still employed in their workshops had to pay "trade taxes." The finance commission evaluated every separate tax for each taxpayer. Every Jew who made use of the aid committee was pelted with tax notices. In addition, the German tax office demanded taxes, which every citizen had to pay.

p. 83

The circle of taxes turned faster and stronger. Great sums of money flowed into the *Judenrat* treasury. However, thousands of complaints came in from those who could not bear the heavy tax load. Friction arose between the appraisal commission and the taxpayers. The finance commission sent inspectors out into the city who had to investigate the exact situation of each payer. Many "tax payers" became receivers of support because it was shown that they had been hungry for a long time because they could not bring themselves to turn to the aid committee for support. A "higher appraisal commission" was created to consider the complaints of the payers. For some, the tax sum was lowered; for others they were increased still more.

However, there were also difficulties in paying, and once, when the *Judenrat* treasury was empty and there was nothing with which to cover the outlays, the *Judenrat* presented the regime with a list of those who had not paid their taxes.

One early morning, gendarmes in autos arrived unexpectedly in the Jewish neighborhoods and arrested those who had not paid their taxes during the required terms. If the husband was not in the house, they took the wife. Those arrested were taken outside of the city and, even though it was then winter, they were placed in a large stall. Only after three weeks, when a large part of the demanded taxes was paid and a guarantee was given for the remaining sum, were the arrestees released.

The Germans transformed the *Judenrat* into an instrument for extracting whatever they wanted from the Jewish population.

The *Judenrat* once received an order to bring the most expensive children's toys to the "city authorities." It turned out that an excursion for German children to the eastern areas that were occupied by the Germans had been organized in Germany. The children were supposed to receive toys when they would pass our city. The *Judenrat* had looked in the shops and could not find the appropriate things. When the city chief learned of this, he telephoned the *Judenrat*, saying that if the toys did not appear during the course of several hours, the chairman of the *Judenrat* himself should report to him. The most able clerks were immediately sent out, who made a search of the Jewish businesses and private residences of the former rich men, and took everything that was available.

p. 84

The toys were promptly delivered on deadline to the city chief and German women went to the train station and the children traveling through were given the presents. At the same time, Jewish children cried their eyes out for their toys.

* *
*

The Germans regularly imposed themselves on Jewish labor like parasites and exploited the Jews in every way.

They began to visit the Jewish craftsmen.

The president of the *Judenrat* and the Jews who performed gyrations in the German offices, informed the Germans about who was the best tailor, shoemaker, lingerie maker, and so on. The Germans and their wives began to visit these craftsmen and order work from them. The Jewish craftsmen gladly received the German "clients," in the hope of, through them, being able to better their bitter fate a little. The Germans ordered work from the best artisans and contemptuously threw them several small coins for the finished work so that it would appear that they had paid. The Jewish craftsmen endeavored that the work they did for the Germans would be the best. The German "clients" were delighted by the work of the Jews. The "chief of the city" was clothed by the best Jewish tailor in the city, who would use the opportunity to ask for a favor for himself or for a Jew who found himself with some hardship, while measuring for a beautiful suit or fur, and sometimes in this manner he was successful.

p. 85

The German women also found the best Jewish tailor of women's clothing and had him sew their new clothing. They understood that it was more worthwhile for them to come accompanied by their husbands to the Jewish tailors, who would want to ask for a favor and therefore would do the work for free.

And thus it was with all of the other Jewish craftsmen who sewed and clothed the Germans from head to foot, both military men and civilians and their wives and children. They were freed of the terror that was administered to the Jewish population.

In time the *Judenrat* also began to make use of the acquaintance of the craftsmen with the Germans in order to cause the repeal of severe decrees against individual Jews or for the entire community. In several cases the craftsmen worked for their "clients" entirely without pay and the *Judenrat* provided the cloth.

Hope arose that perhaps through the craftsmen a few of the troubles that the Jewish population had to endure could be successfully alleviated.

p. 86

Chapter XVI

The "Aryanization" of Jewish Businesses

The Gestapo, the gendarmerie, the city leadership with its officials and all other Germans and *Folks-Deutschn*, who were in our city in large numbers, lived a good life. They found themselves far from the war's front line and they tried to arrange the best and most beautiful for themselves. One day they organized to create businesses that would serve only Germans.

This "creation of German businesses" happened in a very "simple" way: German officials, accompanied by gendarmes, barged into a Jewish business and drove out the employees. Then they took the owner for a short interrogation; they wanted to know where the money, the goods and everything that belonged to the business was. The books were looked through superficially; the money in the cashbox was counted and taken and the owner had to give away the keys and everything that he had with him. If he asked questions, "How come, where is the justice," he immediately received an answer that he would then remember for a long time. They immediately went from the business to the merchant's private residence and if they found goods, the residence was requisitioned with everything found there. Thus the owner of a large business became a thoroughly poor man in the course of one hour.

The looted businesses were handed over to a German or a *Folks-Deutsch*. The Jewish name was torn off the sign and there appeared in the German language: *Hier wird verkauft nur fur Deutsch* [Only Germans may buy here]. The new German merchant sold the goods that the Jew had left. He received permission to requisition the products from the nearby peasants for which he paid very little.

In the "Aryanized" businesses, the German population acquired goods and food products at very reduced prices. For instance, two kilos of bread, for which the entire population paid 30 *zlotys*, cost the Germans only one *zloty*; the Germans paid six *zlotys* for a kilo of butter that cost 200 *zlotys*. And so on for other articles.

p. 87

The new "merchants" received wide opportunities to carry out new businesses: They took the goods away for the lowest prices; a small amount they sold for low earnings and they sold the remainder on the black market for higher prices.

Polish officials, seeing the German businesses with the cheap prices, also wanted to have such businesses. They proceeded to open stores. However, in order to acquire premises, Jews were again thrown out of their shops and the premises were "Aryanized." The stores also received part of their food products for cheap prices.

During the "Aryanization action" the Germans would be seen going through the Jewish streets with lead pencils and notebooks in their hands and recording Jewish businesses. An hour later, the owner of the recorded shop would receive a notice from the "city leadership" to leave the premises. The large white boards with the blue *Mogen Dovid* [Star of David] in the window and at the entrance of the Jewish businesses made it easy to locate the Jewish premises. The *Folks-Deutschn* and Poles also searched Jewish shops and if they had connections in the German offices, the Jewish owners would be thrown out and they would take over the business.

The Jewish manufacturing, finished furniture, linen and haberdashery businesses were liquidated all at once and in the following manner:

One morning all of the businesses were attacked simultaneously by gendarmes. The owners and the employees were driven out, the premises were locked, the windows and doors were sealed and the keys were taken.

p. 88

The shops remained locked for several weeks; the merchants tried to get the *Judenrat* to intervene. However, no one could help. The matter ended after long weeks in this way:

Before the war, a Polish officer named Maszewicz lived in our city. The officer died and left a wife and son and daughter. The family remained without means and lived in need. Mrs. Maszewiczreceived the position of selling lottery tickets. However, this business brought her only a little income and in addition, it reached the point where the wife and two children, wanting to commit suicide, took poison. But they were saved. Nothing more was heard about this family.

When the Germans entered our city, we first began to see Mrs. Maszewicz often in the company of the city chief, Dr. Wendler. It became know that the woman was descended from a family from Germany; she was a *Folks-Deutsch*. Mrs. Maszewicz began to travel around in her own auto; she opened two large textile businesses in the most beautiful neighborhood in the city and received control of the largest Jewish factories that had already been "Aryanized" and, in general, she became known as the right hand of the city chief. Mrs. Maszewicz would often do a favor for a Jew and sometimes visited the chairman of the *Judenrat*. In time, this woman became the most influential person in the city.

After being closed for several weeks, the Jewish manufacturing businesses were all opened again and the transfer of their goods to Mrs. Maszewicz's businesses began. Jewish workers labored for many weeks transferring great quantities of goods in trucks under police supervision.

p. 89

The Jewish merchants stood from afar with grieving hearts and watched as all of their goods were taken from the businesses and they were not permitted even to go closer to their business premises.

The emptied premises on the most attractive streets were given to the Germans, while the keys to the other shops were given to the *Judenrat*. Again, the *Judenrat*, which always made use of an opportunity to extract money, gave the keys only to those owners who paid a great sum of money. A small number of merchants took back their business premises with the payment of money, and most businesses were auctioned and whoever paid the most money received the premises. The former large manufacturing businesses were converted into small shops selling soda water, ice, toys, buttons, cheap fruit and so on.

Chapter XVII

Liquidation of the Jewish Factories

The large Jewish factories within the firm "Gnaschiner Manufaktur" in Czenstochow, which employed several thousand people before the war, were located outside the city on the road to the German border. When the German military marched by the factory on the second day of the war, a tall, long-time factory official went out to greet the Germans with flowers. This official, who was known as a Pole for many years, was suddenly transformed into a *Folks-Deutsch* and was chosen by the Germans to head the factory.

Jewish master craftsmen, factory officials and the chief engineer lived in the factory houses.

p. 90

All of the Jews were no longer permitted to work and the new manager threw them out of their apartments, not permitting them to take even the least trifle of their possessions with them. The newly revealed German also denounced the owner, as he took the money and the cashbox from him. The owner had to endure a great deal and in the end had to leave the city.

The same thing happened with the foreign owned factories, French, Belgian and others, with which Germany was at war. The "trustees" taking over their offices began their activities by checking if the original owners had left everything in "order." If the cash box agreed with the books, if the money had been taken out of the banks and if the stock of raw and manufactured goods were in accord with the books. If something appeared not to be in order the Jewish owner was called to the "trustee" at the factory and was murderously beaten there, then he was taken for interrogation and had to answer the questions posed. Manufacturers who had sent their goods deeper into the country several weeks before the war in order to safeguard them against all possibilities had to inform the "trustee" and bring the goods back at their own cost.

The greatest number of "trustees" were former officials from the same factories. They were even worse than the new unfamiliar "trustees." Not wanting to be associated with the owner and former working colleagues, they immediately drove away all of the Jews and hung out an inscription at the entrance, "Jews are now forbidden to enter." A former official, who had been sent at the owner's expense to England in order to study the weaving trade, became the "trustee" of the Jewish factory, Warta. After taking over the leadership of the factory, he immediately drove out the Jews on the first day. This same person also took over the Juta Factory, which he liquidated, sold the goods and the machines and thereby earned many millions. The former Jewish director of the factory, who remained without means of support, asked him for help. However, instead of help, he took his watch from him and laughed at him.

p. 91

And this is how all Jews were handled, both owners and employees and workers at the factories taken over by the Germans. A small exception was a number of smaller factories and shops, where the owners were themselves tradesmen and managed the enterprise. The new manager, the "trustee," did not feel himself capable of running the enterprise and, therefore, they left the owner at work. It should be understood that work in such conditions was bitter for the Jews, but one could not refuse. In addition, he would have had to work at forced labor somewhere in a forest or in the water, if not at the factory.

However, the earnings of the Jewish workers who were permitted to stay in their positions were 25% lower than what the non-Jewish workers earned. In addition, the non-Jewish workers received certain products that the Jewish workers did not receive.

The Jewish factories operated for a long time using the raw materials that the owners had left. A number of factories had enough raw materials for two years. The new money that the Germans had introduced did not win the trust of the population. Therefore, every one wanted to protect themselves with goods. Polish merchants paid any price for a little merchandize. The "trustees" of the factories were required to sell goods at the pre-war prices, but they took ten times the price and listed the normal prices in the books, so that these people made millions in a very short time.

p. 92

The Jews, from whom the factories were taken, and who had not been left with any work, turned to the central regime with a request that they receive support from the revenue, because they did not have the means with which to live. After a long time, the regime informed the "trustees" that they should pay the owners 200 *zlotys* a month, but with the stipulation that the support did not have to come from capital, if the enterprise had "superfluous" expenses. The payment of these 200 *zlotys* thus became dependent on the "good will" of the "trustees," who always found a reason for not paying the money, although in three day's earnings, there was enough under the current conditions. The 200 *zlotys* were also – with a few exceptions – not paid. There were only a small number of "trustees" who also "thought about the future" when the war would end and in each case wanted to remain on good terms with the owners of the enterprises. They also understood that the co-workers of the former owners would be of more use than the new personnel who had no knowledge in the field of work. These owners, although they worked at simple jobs, actually stayed in close contact with the "trustees." They showed the "trustees" the entire mechanism of the business and shared in the income.

In time, the raw materials that the Jewish owners had accumulated were depleted. The government had allocated new material in small quantities and, more generally, not at all, because everything was provided for the ammunition factories. The enterprises were shut down little by little. The regime decreed that several firms be consolidated into one enterprise. However, the new firms did not last long and had to be liquidated because of shortages of raw materials. The machines from the Jewish factories were sent away somewhere and a large amount was used as scrap in the iron smelters, so as to be made over into artillery guns or other weapons.

p. 93

*   *
*

Not only shops and factories, but also housing was taken from the Jews and they were placed under a "trustee manager." An office was created under the name *treuhandschaft fir yidishn grundbesitz* [trusteeship for Jewish real property]. A specialist in housing management, who was for many years an administrator for Jewish homeowners in Dartmund, was brought from Germany. This person immediately instructed that he be called "doctor" and he settled down in complete comfort as did every civilian and military person in our city. He ordered first that he be given a villa that the *Judenrat* had to beautifully furnish. Then he had to be provided with a renovated and appropriately furnished office of several rooms and then he began his "activity." His deputy and the remaining personnel were Poles from Pozen – this was a special type of Pole who always had had a reputation for anti-Semitism. The administration of the Jewish houses was given to the *Folks-Deutschn* and Poles. Each of them received an entire street of houses and they began to collect rent. The books for the houses were organized and the past sums of rent owed from before the war had to be paid by the tenants to the last *groshn*. The Jewish homeowners had to pay rent just as every other tenant.

p. 94

The press began to write about the bad condition of the Jewish houses that were taken over by the German "trustees" and their assistants. The houses were supposed to be renovated under the management of the Germans. However, in the end, the opposite happened. The new administration only extorted still more money from the tenants and the houses now actually were neglected.

The administrators, the *Folks-Deutschn*, carried out searches in the Jewish residences and took everything that had any worth, on the pretext that it fell under requisition orders. In this way they would take out machines and goods from small factories. They did this after eight o'clock at night when Jews were forbidden to be in the street and they could not see to where everything was being taken away. One audacious Jew, from whom the administrator had taken out his entire possessions at night, informed the police and showed the Polish firm to which everything had been taken. The Polish police carried out an investigation and showed that everything matched exactly as had been declared: that the Pole had purchased the goods and the machines stolen from the entire factory from the administrator. All of the things were sealed and as the administrator was a *Folks-Deutsch*, the Polish police could not make a decision on the matter and the Jew went to the Gestapo. In a few days, the Jew and his son received an invitation to appear at the Gestapo. They went with light hearts, in the complete certainty they would not put any blame on them.

However, the two Jews were received with murderous blows and hurled into a cellar as soon as they entered the Gestapo office. After lying there for several hours, from there they were taken to the second floor into a room where their administrator was waiting for them. Again, he and a Gestapo person beat the father and son so badly that they lay unconscious. When they were revived with a pail of cold water, it was declared that "Jewish swindlers" must not blame the German people for anything.

p. 95

After a certain amount of time it was just possible to extract the two Jews from the Gestapo. They lay in bed for a long time until they recovered after the murderous blows. This was a lesson for all of the Jews that they should not complain against the Germans and *Folks-Deutschn*. The administrator continued to remain in his post and the Jew paid rent to him for his residence in his own house.

Chapter XVIII

"Care for Culture"

The *Judenrat* received an order from the regime that the buildings that had earlier been the location of the Jewish hospital had to be made into a dormitory and a school for German children. All of the premises there had to be renovated, all auditoriums, rooms and entrances had to be renewed; the large garden had to be beautified with new plants and everything had to be organized "as was appropriate for a German school."

The technical division of the *Judenrat* mobilized all of its strength; the labor office employed the necessary number of workers and the building of the new "German" work began, which lasted for many weeks and cost the *Judenrat* a great deal of money.

p. 96

The representative of the chief of the city monitored the work. During his visits, as a reward for their work, he would curse the Jews with the worst words. When the renovation was finished, beautiful furniture and all the other requirements needed for a modern dormitory were brought in. The *Judenrat* delivered the required manufactured goods, from which the Jewish tailors sewed uniforms for the students who were already assigned to be in the dormitory.

While the Jewish tradesmen were still employed doing the last work and in preparing the decorations for the opening celebration, it was learned that the governor of the Radom district was coming to the opening. The representative of the city chief with his whip in his hand arrived several hours early. He looked around to see if everything was in order and called out: "Jews disappear!" His whip began to fall over the heads of the Jewish workers and he beat them until all of the Jews were driven away.

Dread reigned in the city when the governor arrived there. Jews were not allowed to leave their houses. The streets were guarded by police and, there, in the former Jewish hospital building, the grandest holiday took place. The next day we read in the newspapers that the governor gave a fiery speech and thanked the German officers of the National Socialist Party for the new, beautiful work that they had done in the neighboring land of the German Reich.

The Jewish police office in the small ghetto

Jews in large ghetto

A short time later, the chairman of the *Judenrat* was called to the city chief, who told him that each institution and firm in our city would have to give a one-time large monetary payment for the further development of the dormitory and the *Judenrat* also had to make a contribution for this purpose. The chairman of the *Judenrat* understood that this "friendly offer" must not be refused and announced a contribution of 50,000 *zlotys* for the dormitory for the Hitler children. The chairman wondered from where the money would come. However, the "city chief" felt insulted that the chairman had announced such a small sum for such an important purpose. The chairman tried to explain the scarcity of money and promised to increase the sum and the *Judenrat* had sufficient work to procure the sum for this "voluntary contribution."

p. 97

*   *
*

Not much time passed and the *Judenrat* received an order to provide a swimming pool for the German population in our city. A sports room also had to be created with all of the modern accommodations. In addition, the city theater that was built just before the war had to be completed.

The best Jewish artisans again worked for many months; the best Jewish sportsmen with hundreds of workers poured out their sweat working on the fields. The inauguration of each particular institution took place with great solemnity in the presence of highly placed German personalities who, in solemn speeches, praised the great and difficult achievements the Germans with their professional capabilities had carried out in this "neglected country." The party members and the officials of the city chief's regime received great awards and furloughs for their great exertions so that they could rest a little from their hard work.

Chapter XIX

Extermination

The Gestapo rummaged through the remaining archives and examined all of the materials from which they could record the names of "political suspects" or anti-fascists, both those who were Jews and those who were Polish. They mainly searched for the intelligentsia. Arrests took place every day and every night. People were placed in prison and, after a short time, they generally disappeared. The residents of the village, Olsztyn, not far from a forest, were able to relate that people were being taken from the prison to the woods during the early morning hours; there they were forced to dig pits into which they were then flung and there shot.

p. 98

Food brought by the relatives of the arrestees was accepted twice a week at the prison. The food was often returned with the explanation that their relative was no longer in the prison. The wives of those men who disappeared then began going from one office to another in order to learn the fate of the person who had suddenly disappeared. Finally, they received a severe answer, that they should stop taking an interest in where their husbands are. Always, therefore, when women or children came to the prison with food for their husbands or fathers, they would stand in fear and wait; would they bring back the food or not? The secrets of the Olsztyner forest were no longer a secret and returned food meant the relative no longer was alive.

Therefore, a heartbreaking lament often was heard on the prison street. Wives and children or parents of those who had suddenly disappeared threw themselves on the ground in despair, tore at their hair and screamed in wild voices. The gendarmes immediately chased them with rifle butts. The relatives of the arrestees would wait the entire night for the autos that took their dearest to the Olsztyner forest. From afar – because one was not permitted to go near – they would stand and see how before daylight, the prison street would suddenly be surrounded by the Gestapo and people were loaded into autos driven right up to the gate. When the autos drove by the road on which the relatives of the arrested stood, a cry would break out and the relatives accompanied the autos as if following a funeral.

p. 99

Every few days prisoners would be sent out to concentration camps. After every transport, the prison would again be filled with new arrestees and thus the procedure continued constantly with arrests and deportations. It was learned that there was a concentration camp in the town of Oswiecim [Auschwitz in German] not far from Krakow to which thousands of people were continually brought and, after a short time, annihilated. The families of the people sent there received a telegram that their relative had "died." After a while, the family was called to the Gestapo where they were given some of the deceased's clothing.

The relatives of the deported made an effort at various offices to save those closest to them from Auschwitz. However, it was quickly learned that those for whom the efforts were made for their release perished more quickly and the families immediately received a telegram, "has died."

Yet, two or three people were found in the city who had returned from the Auschwitz Concentration Camp. Special efforts had been made for them through people with great influence. In general, how they were freed, what happened in the camp, remained a secret because they did not relate even one word about it all. They were warned that if they said anything, they would be sent back.

In the summer of 1940 all of the Jewish lawyers were arrested in the city. They were placed in the prison cells where those chosen to be sent to Auschwitz were held. The families of the lawyers made every effort to save them. The *Judenrat* also tried to do something and Wajnrib was much occupied with the matter. At first, the actions to save everyone were carried out jointly. Later, each family began separately to do everything possible because of fear that they would be sent away and help would come too late.

p. 100

After several days it was learned that the Gestapo had arrested more Jews from various classes. Their families also ran to the *Judenrat* and to Wajnrib to beg that something be done for them. They wanted to give everything that they possessed, but no one wanted to do anything for them. They were sent to Auschwitz several days later.

Right after this, the lawyers were freed. It was suspected that the lawyers were saved at the expense of the other arrestees, for whom no one wanted to intervene. If this was how it was, it remained a secret. In each case, the families of the deported went around with darkened hearts and with anger at the *Judenrat*, whom they suspected of making this terrible exchange. The suspicion was also strong because the lawyers gave the *Judenrat* a great deal of money that was required for the release. Meanwhile, new arrests were occurring; new transports again went to Oswiecim and telegrams were again received from the Auschwitz Concentration Camp to the wives that their husbands had "died."

Chapter XX

Ghetto

Various rumors arose that a ghetto would be introduced with separate parts for Jews and a separate one for "Aryans," as had been introduced some time ago in Warsaw and other cities.

p. 101

These rumors caused a panic and people ran to the *Judenrat* to learn about the matter. The chairman and the other members of the *Judenrat* calmed and reassured everyone that "with us such a thing cannot happen, because we are giving the Germans everything that they demand of us." However, the rumors very quickly turned out to be correct.

There was a German "housing office" in our city that had the assignment of creating residences for the Germans who came here. The administrator of this office was a German named Linderman. Linderman was a frequent visitor to the Jewish craftsmen who would do various work for him and his wife without payment or at half price as they would do for other German officials from whom they could expect some kind of favor.

And once a Jewish tailor measuring the manager in the housing office for a beautiful suit cautiously asked how things were going with the ghetto. The German answered that "they are going very well" and that a meeting would need to take place soon with the leaders of the city about "organizing a special district for you Jewish residents."

The panic grew when this news became known. In time, people wanted to provide a roof over their heads. Small wagons began to move furniture and things from the elegant street to the poor part of the city, where the Jews assumed the ghetto would be located. Other wagons again went with things from the Jewish streets to the Polish neighborhoods – these were Jews taking their things to "Polish friends" to hide "until the times would change."

p. 102

However, the city leader quickly issued a decree that no furniture or other things could be transported from one place to another without special permission. It became clearer from this decree that the ghetto would soon be instituted. Therefore, there was great confusion. People wanted to save what they could of their possessions. Men, women and children went back and forth to the Jewish streets dozens of times and carried away clothing which they wore and other things that they were able to carry with them to their relatives. In the same way, others would take away their things from the Jewish neighborhoods to the Poles of their acquaintance.

Jewish carpenters received an order to make large wooden signs on which inscriptions had to be made that Jews were forbidden to go farther under the threat of the death penalty.

It was immediately learned that the housing office at the *Judenrat* would assign residences for the Jews who were moved from the "Aryan" part of the city into the "Jewish housing district." This Jewish ghetto was already decided upon and a period of five days was given for the move.

Polish police were placed at the entrance of the streets that were designated as the ghetto. Jews were not permitted to leave to enter the Aryan streets. The number of residences in the ghetto streets and the number of "Aryans" who had to leave the ghetto was received. A housing office was created for the Polish population that had to leave the ghetto streets, which allotted residences in the "Aryan" part of the city in which Jews had lived until then.

There was a great crowd in front of the Jewish housing office. Those driven out of the "Aryan side" wanted to have a small piece of roof over their head. The assigning of residences went very slowly. Chosen as chairman of the Jewish housing office was a young man named Kojlnbrener. This Kojlnbrener came from Gdynia and succeeded in making the acquaintance of German officers here, who ordered the *Judenrat* to give this young man a job. This is how he became the "chief" of the housing office and in his hands lay the distribution of residences. This "housing chief" had no set office hours and he never hurried when Jews stood in long lines and waited to obtain a small piece of roof over their head.

p. 103

In the end the ghetto was established. Jewish workers dug holes in all corners of the ghetto and erected large yellow-colored signs at which Jewish painters stood and painted an inscription in German, Polish and Yiddish: "Jews who leave the Jewish housing district will be punished with the death penalty; "Aryans" who enter the Jewish housing district with the purpose of trading with or buying from Jews will be punished by imprisonment."

In April, two days before the Christian holiday of Easter, all of the Jews in our city, Czenstochow, began living together without "Aryans" in the ghetto. Yet, our ghetto was still different from the ghettos in other cities. There were no walls and no fences. The Polish population was not permitted to trade with Jews, but they were permitted to go through the ghetto. Our city was built in such a way that the 40,000 Jews could not be enclosed and the "Aryan" population" could not be prevented from entering the ghetto streets. This gave us the hope that our ghetto would not be completely closed in and we would not be exposed to hunger as in the other cities.

When all of the Jews were already living in the ghetto, a small number of Jews still remained on the "Aryan side" for a short time. These were the Jewish craftsmen who had been chosen, who had to work for the Germans. And as it happened to be the Christian holiday, the Jewish workers were very busy with work for the Germans. They had to finish furniture for the holiday and moving to the ghetto would have delayed the work. Therefore, the Jewish workshops were permitted for a time to remain on the "Aryan side." This way done, it should be understood, for the comfort of the Germans and not as a favor to the Jews. When a gendarme entered a fashion shop, Rena, and ordered that the premises be closed as were other Jewish businesses in this area, the owner wanted to follow the order immediately. However, the German women who were waiting for their hats went to their husbands, high officials in the city leadership and created a stir: What do you mean their hats would not be ready for the holiday! Therefore, an order was issued that the shop should remain open until the Germans provided other premises. The only Jewish business, with a large Jewish star hanging in the window, remained open in the most beautiful neighborhood in the city. It was soon learned that the regime had assigned a special house near the ghetto for the best Jewish craftsmen who were working for the Germans, so that the German clients would not be forced to enter the ghetto.

p. 104

*　　*

*

The first morning in the ghetto:

The people went out on the streets very early to look around and see where they were. They began to go through the streets, but there was not much free area. There were boundaries all over; large signs with inscriptions, by which stood Jewish *ordnungsmener* [police] dressed in red hats with shiny visors. The white *juden-band* [arm band with the Jewish star] on the right arm, the *ordnungsband* [police arm band] on the left arm, armed with rubber sticks just as the real policemen. Many passages to the various streets were not part of the ghetto and the people began to orient themselves, where they could go and where they could not go. Movement became more difficult and the streets narrower. One person pushed another while moving on the sidewalk and the policemen did not permit anyone to go in the middle of the street. The workers hurried to their assembly places. They banged on the stone sidewalks with their wooden shoes and made noise. They marched in groups with their brigade leaders to the new border of the ghetto. The Jewish policemen showed with their rubber sticks that they should remain standing. The brigade leader and his group stood and were not permitted to go through as usual. The same thing happened at all of the borders of the ghetto. The Jewish workers office gave out provisional passes allowing the workers to go outside of the ghetto to their workplaces. The policemen counted every group and let them pass.

p. 105

The Polish population went in and out of the ghetto and the Jewish police had no authority over them. The Poles were not allowed to stop on the Jewish streets, which were only a way of transit for them. They thought over the new situation and had short conversations with their Jewish acquaintances. Each had something to take care of with the other; here and there a Jew asked a favor of a Polish acquaintance, that he obtain something from the "Aryan side."

Jews stood at the ghetto boundaries and looked over to the "Aryan" side," to the lucky people who could move freely, go where they wanted to, to travel by train, by auto, wherever they wanted to go. The Polish population also looked over to us with strange looks. They looked with facial expressions as if we were infected with an epidemic illness and must be isolated, or as if we were half-wild people. We felt how much the Germans had lowered us in the eyes of the Poles.

Jews carried bricks, lime and sand through the streets in order to wall in the courtyards that half belonged to the Jewish side. Walls and gates were opened in order to create new passageways; people crawled through holes and over mounds so that they could enter their residences.

p. 106 and 107

Long lines of people stood in front of the housing office. They were not satisfied with their new residences; others could not get along with their new neighbors. It was crowded; the house was wet; it rained in and people came there with other such reasons. Merchants, who had lost their business premises on the "Aryan" side of the city, stood for hours at the *Judenrat* and tried to obtain premises in the ghetto that the "Aryans" had left. The *Judenrat* asked for a great deal of money for premises. There was a clamor, a racket. A merchant yelled, "How is it possible? From where would I get the money? I was ruined, gave up my business, I now live in a small room without any economic means, I must pay your taxes and now you demand new thousands for a small shop! If I do not have a shop, I will not be able to pay any taxes." However, the *Judenrat* was accustomed to such arguments and they were no longer answered. A second person and a third were soon there. The number of shops was limited and those interested in them were many.

Small shops were quickly opened in larger premises in which there were previously large businesses. Now there was a little haberdashery, buttons, electrical things, a few food products, and sweets. The former large merchants became used to small stores for which the *Judenrat* took large payments.

Deeper in the ghetto, farther down near the old market, there was a noise, a stir: Jewish children, boys and girls, yelled out their goods with their already hoarse throats: saccharine, ersatz tea, yarn for sewing, soap, etc. Each child wanted to out shout the others. Passing Jews and Poles bought on the run because trading was not permitted there. A Jewish policeman standing there drove the "merchants" away in a relaxed manner. When a Polish policeman approached, the Jewish policeman became vigorous. The sellers ran away quickly through the nearby gate and the Poles continued walking as if they had not bought or sold anything here. Some of the customers took the opportunity to leave without having paid for the goods. The small businessmen chased after them. Meanwhile, the gendarme came and chased the sellers. There was turmoil and running on all sides, everyone escaped. However, when the gendarme caught one, he took all of the goods and "paid" for them with blows. When the gendarmes left, the "dealing" started up again. The "merchants" did not stop for anything. Need and hunger drove them and there were no other possibilities to earn a little bread. Children were stationed on every corner of the selling square who knew each gendarme and Polish policeman, even when they were dressed in civilian clothing. The children had a special nickname for each of the policemen and gendarmes. Once a boy "on watch" shouted: "*Gargl geyt, tsi up* [The throat is coming, withdraw]!" This meant that the tall gendarme who had a long neck was coming and it was necessary to "withdraw," that is, escape. After such a signal, the entire square was emptied in the course of seconds. In a short time, the "merchants" again moved out of their hiding places. It did not last long and again a signal was heard: "*Der fesele geyt* [The little keg is coming]!" This meant that the short gendarme with a thick stomach was coming. Later, again a scream was heard: "*Der veyser kop – vert a hoz* [The white head – become a hare]!" This meant that the gendarme with a white head of hair was coming and one had to become "a hare," that is, escape. Then again an alarm: "*Der royter fuks – makh fis* [The red fox, run]!" "The red fox" was the nickname of a Polish policeman with a red face. The Jewish children had great trouble from him. He hit them with a rubber stick and then took them to the police commissariat where they were tortured anew by other murderers like him.

p. 108

Among many others, there was a gendarme of whom the boys shouted: "The murderer is here!" This was a person dressed in civilian clothes with a truly murderous face. With one hand he caught one seller and with the second another and kicked them both with his feet. Meanwhile, the others escaped.

In this way, the Jewish children in the ghetto protected themselves from their persecutors.

Chapter XXI

Lost Souls

There were various types who were conspicuous in the ghetto streets of our city:

A man in his fifties with a respectable appearance was often seen. He would always go alone with his head down, a white band on his right arm. He was known by the name, Lavendel. He never dreamed he would be found among Jews. In general, he was not a Jew. His connection to Judaism was only through his grandfather, who was a Christian convert. It was not known earlier in the city that he was descended from Jews. This Lavendel was the agent for the Belgian Electrical Society and was always a severe and unsympathetic person in taking care of the interests of his office. And here, he had also been driven into the ghetto with all of the Jews where he had no acquaintances and felt strange and lonely. The tragedy the man was living through was always visible on his pensive and dejected face. It was also said that the officials, who had worked under his leadership for many years, had pointed out his Jewish heritage.

p. 109

The magistrate of the county court was named Geizler. He was the son of a rich Jewish proprietor. The magistrate, Geizler, and his wife and children had converted several years earlier in order for him to be able to become a magistrate in the Polish court. He was disconnected from Jewish society for a long time and entered the "better" Polish society. However, the Germans sent him over from the "Aryan side" to the ghetto, where he walked with quick steps from one border of the ghetto to another and everywhere read the same inscriptions on the large signs. He remained standing in front of the sign for a minute, spit and, again, began to walk back. He gave the impression of a fox that had been fooled into a cage from which he could not extract himself.

*   *

*

With a *juden-band* [armband with the Star of David required to be worn by Jews] on her arm, the wife of the well-known lawyer, Gruczinski, was often seen going through the ghetto streets. Mrs. Gruczinski converted 20 years ago in order to marry the Pole. When the Germans entered our city, the lawyer, Gruczinski, finally found the right moment to get rid of the Jewish woman and he drove her out of the house He married a younger and prettier real "Aryan" from a rich Polish family. The lawyer's former wife, driven from her husband and from the "Aryan side," went through the ghetto streets lonely and desperate. Sometimes, she stopped her former Jewish women acquaintances from who she looked for a little sympathy. Her Jewish parents were also here in the ghetto, but she did not live with them, but with a former childhood friend. The once pretty woman had a dejected, gloomy face, with eyes that cried out grief and fear. She carried around a basket with pieces of soap and other trifles, which she sold to Jewish women who had compassion for her and with the earnings strove to manage in order not to die of hunger.

p. 110

There was a woman of German origin who led a peaceful family life with a Jew for twenty-two years. They had to leave their residence long ago. Her husband was in the ghetto and she on the "Aryan side." She brought him a little food every day. However, she was afraid to go upstairs to his apartment. She turned here and there until an opportune moment appeared; she ran up the stairs that led to her husband's residence. They owned a factory and as there was a danger of it being requisitioned because of its Jewish owner, they formally divorced and she, the pure "Aryan," became the owner of the factory and all of the remaining possessions. She helped her "divorced" husband with what she was able, but she had to be sure that no one learned of it.

*   *

*

The old, grey, but very elegant Abramson was often seen in the street. He was the representative of the large raw material factory for dozens of years. He was very beloved by the Jewish population and by the factory owners with whom he carried on business. He married a German woman from Vienna 30 years ago and she converted to Judaism. They had two sons. Their life was broken after the Germans entered our city. Abramson did not want his wife and children to suffer because of him and he left for the ghetto, leaving his family as Germans on the "Aryan" side. This also was not easy for them. He wife came every day to the ghetto with pots of food for her beloved husband. Each son also separately smuggled himself into the ghetto for a short time to [visit] his old father, watching carefully to be sure that no one noticed.

*   *

*

On the first tree-lined street near the border of the ghetto stood the engineer, Fajnkind, every evening after work in the technical division of the *Judenrat*. He waited for his Christian wife with whom he lived together for many years. Now he was in the ghetto and she on the "Aryan side." She came to him every night and they poured out their hearts in the middle of the street. When a policeman neared, they parted as if strangers.

p. 111

* *
*

A man of 50 once stopped me in the street with a "*gut morgn* [good morning]" in German. I was lucky and saw a familiar face. I remembered that we had met in the barracks when the Germans seized Jews on the street and imprisoned them there.

We carried out a conversation about the situation and the man strangely heaved a heavy sign. I asked him what was the matter and he answered that his mood was so heavy that he had to speak to someone from his heart.

And he told me his history:

"I left our city, Czenstochow, for Germany 24 years ago for the city of Cologne on Rhine. I was a good metal engraver and found work there immediately, earned well and lived very well.

"I met a pretty German girl, married her and lived a very nice life. We gave our two sons a good upbringing and we lived happily and content until Hitler came to power. I then realized that I would no longer be able to live quietly with my family in Germany and decided to return to the city of my birth, to Czenstochow. I came here with my family, set up an engraving shop and earned well. I again lived happily with my family until the Germans came here to us."

p. 112

The man suddenly lost his self-control and burst into tears in the middle of the street. When he calmed himself a little, he further related:

"When the Germans carried out the Bloody Monday in our city, my eldest son and I were forced to go to the barracks with everyone else and after two days were freed from there with others. When the decree was issued that the Jews must wear the bands of shame, my sons and I wore them just as all other Jews. This caused a great deal of pain for my wife. My children suddenly felt that they were Jews and that their mother was a German, a child of the people who were exposing them to shame and mockery. When the law about forced labor was introduced, the *Judenrat* sent my oldest son to a labor camp in Cieszanow. There he was beaten terribly at work by the German murderers and fell dead in the forest. The *Judenrat* informed us that our son was no longer alive. My pain was great. However, I cannot describe the suffering of my wife, who was shocked not only by the heavy blow of losing a child, but by the strange abyss that had suddenly opened for her: she, a German woman, lost her child because he was a Jew and was murdered by the Germans – her brothers. For a short time she found herself in a state that was close to madness. She would go around the entire day and night and scream that she constantly saw her murdered child in front of her eyes and she clung to our second child and pressed him to her heart. Then she fell into a melancholy. A heavy grief settled in our house. We would be quiet entire days and not say one word to each other.

"A German gendarme unexpectedly entered our residence one day. It was my wife's brother. He barely nodded towards me with his head and he called his sister to his side. They spoke for about half an hour. Then he left, not saying goodbye to me. My wife told me that he was a gendarme and was serving in Warsaw.

"From that day on, my wife would go outside to the street. People told me that they often saw her with German train officials. Her brother also began to visit often when I was not in the house. Until one day she declared that she could no longer live with me and that she was going to Warsaw with her brother. Surprised, I ran to her and begged her not to leave me after living together for 25 years. My 11-year old son also could not be pried loose from his mother, the German, and we both fell to her feet and cried. She cried, too, and her tears fell on our heads. She bent down to the ground where my son and I lay and we all heartily hugged, drenching ourselves with hot tears. We rolled on the ground in this way in love and pain until our child fell asleep from exhaustion. Then she suddenly tore herself from the spot with a wild shout, "Stay well," and ran out of the house.

"I lost my beloved wife and my child lost his mother. Now I hang around here in the ghetto like an animal locked in a cage and do not know what to do with myself and my child."

*   *
*

Individual Jews who were employed by the regime on the "Aryan side" as decorators, painters, watchmakers and others tradesmen, *Judenrat* officials and those employed by "Aryan firms" received individual passes from the city managing committee enabling them to leave the ghetto during designated hours of the day to go to their workplaces. The passes were valid for one month and then were exchanged for a second month, if the firm that employed the Jews issued a certificate that the holder would continue to be employed there. Later the city managing committee limited the number of passes; soon people were found who procured the passes for a great deal of money. Jews who had to take care of their business on the "Aryan" side obtained the passes and thus began to revive trade in the ghetto. Jewish merchants secretly joined with Poles, sent them to other cities to buy and sell various goods. They also founded firms with "Aryan" names outside the ghetto and also in other cities. The Poles became partners in the earnings. On the surface everything appeared "Aryan," but actually the commerce was carried out for the most part with Jewish money and Jewish goods. Poles would say that they admired the Jews who despite all of the difficulties and disturbances, carried on their activity with coolness and capability.

p. 114

*   *
*

The German "chief trustee" of non-movable Jewish possessions gave several Jews the right to administer the Jewish houses in the ghetto. All the Jewish houses were divided into the hands of the five or six Jews who the "chief trustee" knew as people who "understood business."

The young man, Kojlnbrener, received the most beautiful houses under his administration and also the franchise to remove the garbage from all of the courtyards in the ghetto. Therefore, all of the remaining Jewish administrators were forced to pay him a monthly fee. He set up his office in one of the houses he administered and all of the tenants promptly paid the rent for the residences, for water, for the sewers that they used, for taking out the garbage, although it always lay in the courtyard.

p. 113

Top: caption, Jews with armbands on Warszawer Street

In the small ghetto

p. 115

The other Jewish administrators also set up their offices where Jews at the appropriate time had to present the rent that flowed to the German trustee as a constant stream of gold. The Jewish administrator understood how to influence his German boss so that no one would complain about the earnings. Therefore, although the tenants constantly ran after them with requests that the roof be repaired because it rained into the residence, the ceiling should be repaired because it posed a danger if it fell down on heads, the administrators paid no attention. They had a German boss who protected them and they were not afraid of anyone. Each tenant had to repair his apartment by himself and the Jewish houses thus became even more neglected.

Chapter XXII

Jewish Police

The Jewish *ordnungsmener* [men who keep order], who in the beginning were occupied with watching the movement in the streets, little by little expanded their activity. They grabbed Jews to work for the Germans and became increasingly strict toward the Jews. The Jewish population, which at first was satisfied with the activity of the *ordnungsmener*, increasingly noticed that the Jewish *ordnungleit* [people keeping order] were infected and corrupted by the Germans. The tone of their brother Jews began to change. A number of the better young people, who could not adapt to the new course, resigned from their posts. Since the ghetto had been created, the Jewish population began to refer to the *ordnungsdinst* [those serving as keepers of order] as "Jewish police." Finally, the "Jewish policemen" reached the point where at each opportunity they let their rubber sticks fall over Jewish heads.

p. 116

The commandant of the Jewish police, Mr. Galster, put on a hat with a white band around it on which four white stars were sewn. Leather was sewn around his pants, as those worn by horsemen. The high officer's boots were clean with a shine like lacquer. In his right hand, he always carried a riding crop with which he made a firm rap against his boot after every few steps. When someone in the street heard the rap behind them, he knew that the officer of the Jewish police was coming.

His friend, Kacinel, the lawyer, was appointed as his general-secretary. He received a police hat with three white officer's star.

The commandant had still other of his friends appointed as police officers and organized the entire police list. When everything was ready, the Jewish police commandant, at the order of the German regime, gathered his men and presented them to the representative of the German regime. The German gendarme officer smiled at the Jewish police commandant, as if as one officer to another, with an ironic smile on his lips and immediately, with an earnest facial expression, turned to the Jewish police and briefed them that they must carry out all of their orders. "If not," he added and pointed to a Gestapo man who was watching the spectacle, "the gentleman with the skull on his hat will take care of you and of all the Jews in the city."

The Jewish police left the spectacle in a not very elevated mood. However, this did not interfere with the arrangements for entertainment in honor of an important event such as the organization of the "Jewish police," and they drank and celebrated until late at night.

p. 117

Two police precincts were opened. One was on the First Avenue under the leadership of Commandant Galster, himself, and the second on Kasze Street under the leadership of Itshe Landau. The police stood at all exits of the ghetto boundaries during the hours when Jews had the right to be on the ghetto streets, and controlled whether the passes were in order. They also paid attention so that, God forbid, Jews did not carry on any trade in the street. They took their office very seriously and chased after the poor traders, even beating them with their rubber sticks. Only a small number of the policemen behaved fairly and with compassion toward the harassed people.

The Jewish labor office often sent lists with the names of those who had not appeared for forced labor. The Jewish police would attack the people at night, taking them out of their beds and placing them in the cellar of their precinct. In the morning, these people were taken to the worst labor.

The German firm *Waserwirtschaft* [Water Industry] ordered the labor office to recruit Jewish workers for it in the shtetl "Nidel," Radomsko district. The firm needed many workers, but no one wanted to go because the conditions were unbearable; it was necessary to stand and work in water. The food was bad and there was no place to sleep. Anyone who could, brought all means to bear not to go there. The labor office demanded that many young men submit for the work and when the time for leaving came, it was seen that many had not appeared. Therefore, when it was decided to send a group, the Jewish police would catch young people in the street a few days earlier and arrest them. The rich would make a payment to the *Judenrat*, which always needed money, and only the poor were sent away to work.

p. 118

The labor office would often receive a command from the German firms or from the regime to provide workers. Then the Jewish police would go out on a hunt, closing off streets, closing gates and they would gather the required number of people, using their rubber sticks, and deliver them to the German work places.

The *Judenrat* would use the Jewish police to collect taxes from those who did not pay promptly, or against those who could not afford to pay the *Judenrat* but who the *Judenrat* did not want to count as poor and thus free from taxes. And the Jewish police would attack these people at night, take them out of their beds and bring them to the police cellars. There they would sit until their families brought the demanded sums to the *Judenrat*. If there were "obstinate" people who still did not take care of the tax accounts, they would be "made softer" through blows. If this also did not help, our *Judenrat* was not ashamed of placing these people in the hands of the German police, who coped with the "obstinate."

The Gestapo also used the Jewish police to find people whom they wished to have in their hands. They would turn to the Jewish police with an ultimatum that they deliver the persons sought and the Jewish police used every means to carry out the Gestapo order.

The Jewish police had the special work of driving the people from the streets. 14,000 people were driven together in an area of a few streets. The ghetto was 400 meters in length and width. The passersby bumped into one another and on summer nights, when the workers returned from work and went out in the streets, in order to breathe more freely, not being able to remain sitting in the small room where they lived with several families, they were driven back to the backstreets, so that they would not be conspicuous. The Germans constantly alerted the *Judenrat* and the police that the Jews were moving around the streets of the ghetto too much. When the work of urging on the people became difficult, particularly during the summer days, the police found a means of doing it. They took the strollers to the police precinct and from there took them to the train station in groups or to certain factories to unload coal from the railway wagons the entire night.

p. 119

On *Shabbos* and Sunday, the coercing through the streets was particularly harsh. The Germans would pay special attention on these two days. Therefore, the police would place a truck and bring the strollers there and then drive them in their holiday clothes away to work. Moreover, this caused people to avoid going through the main streets of the ghetto by any means possible. The people, who were forced to go there because they lived there, would sneak home quickly and unnoticed.

The Jewish police were used by the housing office. The Jewish police intervened if the office had to give someone an order to move to another spot and that person had not done so in time, or if someone did not properly divide a corner in his house with another.

Thus, the Jewish police carried out its work and felt resolute and sure. The leader always moved around in a good mood and was rarely sober. The police precinct looked like a real police office, as if the Jews had autonomy. However, one day the news spread in the ghetto that all of the leaders of the Jewish police had been arrested and sent to forced labor for the German housing office, such as working on the highway.

p. 120

A large crowd went to the housing office to see how those who until then had coerced Jews to forced labor were now themselves working. Many people gathered at the fence of the housing office and watched the spectacle.

No one knew why the leaders of the Jewish police had suddenly lost favor with the Germans. They remained at the housing office doing forced labor for several weeks. They lived in wooden barracks. After great efforts on the part of the *Judenrat*, they were released. However, they did not return to their offices.

The Germans placed two Polish non-commissioned officers in charge of the running of the two Jewish precincts. The Polish leaders established contact with the *Judenrat* with two Jews as liaisons.

Chapter XXIII

Life Goes On

Ershte Aleja [First Avenue], the street going to the train bridge, was allotted to the ghetto. This was achieved through great efforts. All acquaintances of influential Germans were utilized for this purpose. The *Judenrat*, the best Jewish artisans and still other Jews did whatever they could to have *Ershte Aleja* included in the ghetto because this was of great importance for Jews. This was the only convenient street in the ghetto, where large houses were located that could take in many tenants. The apartments here were also larger. Jews knew that without *Ershte Aleja* the ghetto would be very poor. The center of Jewish trade was located on this street. If *Ershte Aleja* remained outside of the ghetto two-thirds of Jewish earnings would have disappeared. The Polish merchants and the Polish city managing committee headed by the mayor did everything to assure that we would receive the *Aleja*. Finally, after great efforts and for a very high price, this street was allocated to the ghetto. And the yellow boards that marked the ghetto boundaries were dug in there on both sides where *Ershte Aleja* ended.

p. 121

The last house on *Ershte Aleja* which bore the number 14 was not assigned to the ghetto. It belonged to the "Aryan" side. This house was one of the most beautiful buildings in our city. It possessed a large and wide entrance with marble steps; beautiful, large and sunny residences with concrete balconies and other comfortable facilities. The owner of the house, a *Folks-Deutsch*, Engineer Artur Franke, was called to the city chief, where it was decreed that 23 Jewish artisans would live in his house that stood right next to the ghetto. This house was fit for the artisans because there was an appropriate entry and residences, suitable for the German clients who would continue to visit the Jewish artisans. This house was cleared of its Polish renters and replacing them were Jewish artisans.

Immediately after the German holiday, Easter, when the ghetto was already in its tragic condition, the furniture and all of the property of the 23 artisans was brought over, of which the German took nothing. The large mirrors for fitting their clients and the armchairs for seating them remained, in order that Germans would be comfortable visiting the Jewish artisans.

The German clients immediately placed orders and the Jewish artisans continued to satisfy them in their new beautiful residences

p. 122

Each master craftsman from a workshop received an appropriate pass from the city leadership that enabled him to move through the entire city because the master craftsmen needed to visit the clients in their residences at their request to be measured for clothing. The Jewish residents of the artisans' house and the journeymen who worked there received passes which permitted them to go into the ghetto and back.

The artisans of the house, *Ershte Aleja* number 14, had comfortable arrangements and lived relatively well. Polish clients, who were happily clothed by the best Jewish artisans, came to the house in addition to the Germans. The artisans charged good prices for these clients.

The artisans used their acquaintance with the Germans in order to help individual Jews who fell into difficulties with the regime. Very often they saved Jews in this manner from the Gestapo. The Jews in the ghetto were happy with the artisans' house at *Aleja* number 14.

German directors of the local textile factories, who were also clothed in the house, had need of tailors to sew men's and women's clothing of paper fabric. Therefore, large quantities of goods were supplied that were divided among the poor Jewish tailors in the ghetto. Later those who were not tailors also started working and earned their livelihood. Hundreds of Jews who had already sold all of their possessions and had no means by which to live were employed in this work.

p. 123

Chapter XXIV

The New War

On the 22nd of June 1941 we saw thousands of cars with cargos of weapons pass by from early in the morning until late at night going in the direction of the German-Russian border established in 1939.

The news was published in the press that a war had broken out between the vast and strong German Reich and weak communist Russia, to which all Jews in the world belong, including, of course, we In Poland.

We immediately felt the war between Germany and Russia in a special way: several days after the war's outbreak, the Gestapo attacked the Jewish residences at night, searching for people based on a prepared register of names of those who belonged to socialist parties before the war. Many of those being looked for were long dead, others were in Russia. However, the Gestapo was not very meticulous with the names or addresses of those found in the attacked residences. Hundreds of people were arrested in this way on that day. After gathering a large number of people, they sent them away to Oswiecim [Auschwitz].

Large posters were nailed up in the ghetto on which it was said that Russian prisoners would be brought through the ghetto and no one should go near, no words should be shouted, nothing including food should be offered them and that whoever violated this would be shot on the spot.

During the course of several days, we saw small groups of the German military accompanied by large dogs arriving by train. It became known that this department would guard the Russian prisoners who were arriving here.

p. 124

Thousand of prisoners arrived by train during the hot summer days. Large units of the German military proceeded in front, driving away all "Aryans" passing by on the sidewalks. All passing "Aryans" were forced to wait until the large mass of prisoners passed through the "Aryan streets."

However, the ghetto streets looked different when the same prisoners were taken through the ghetto streets. Before the march through of the prisoners, the German military units drove the Jewish passersby into the houses. The gates were closed and, if anyone appeared in the windows, shots were fired inside. The streets were empty when the prisoners entered the ghetto; the windows were closed, the gates were locked and it looked like a dead city.

Then, hidden behind the window drapes, several Jews looked out and saw the terrible appearance of the prisoners who passed in long rows. They looked astonished by the emptiness of the streets, while several minutes earlier they had gone through animated streets. They wore wooden shoes on their feet, which banged loudly on the stones as they went. It could be seen on their faces that they were exhausted and starving. Those who fainted and the weak were supported by their colleagues in the rows. Those completely worn out fell down on the stones and those who did not stand up immediately received blows with the butts of the guns and were slid onto wagons that came after from behind.

A German soldier suddenly shouted at a prisoner who walked barefoot and carried his wooden shoes in his hand. The soldier ordered him to put on the shoes. The prisoner using defensive gestures pointed to his wounded feet. A blow with a rifle butt forced the prisoner to put on the shoes.

p. 125

A while later the following scene played out: A man, who was hiding in a small passage between two houses and thought that he would not be seen by anyone, threw out a small package of food to the prisoners. However, a soldier saw it and stabbed him with his bayonet.

Chapter XXV

Mass Hunger

The situation for the Jewish population in the ghetto became more difficult during the winter of 1941-1942. The largest part of the population was badly dressed and did not have the means to buy coal and potatoes. Hundreds of half naked poor people stood in the streets and begged for donations, but no one looked at them.

The winter turned out to be very difficult. There were harsh frosts and deep snow. The thousands of poorly dressed workers would run to their workplaces in their wooden shoes early in the morning. Naked body parts looked out from their torn clothing. The young ones, still children, who worked the entire day in frost and wind, bound their heads with torn kerchiefs. The parents, wives and children of those working remained at home in their lairs, where they starved and froze. The homeless people sat in the asylums on their dark cots, covered with old sacks and rags. In the streets the sellers froze and did not see any customers for their poor little bit of goods. In addition, they were chased and harassed by various persecutors, civilian informers, German, Polish and Jewish policemen.

p. 126

The aid committee made every effort to alleviate the need, but the need was so great that it was impossible to help everyone.

At night the gendarmes would attack the Jewish houses, taking out the men, beating them and taking them beyond the city to clear the highways of snow. They were held there the entire day without food and they came back late at night tired, hungry, bloodied and dispirited. Attacking men at night and dragging them away to clear the snow lasted the entire winter.

In addition to this, fresh troubles appeared: the houses that were at the very edge of the ghetto were attacked at night by German gendarmes who drove out the Jewish residents so quickly that the residents barely had time to get dressed and take something with them. This was done in such a way as to enclose the houses that had been made *Juden-rein* [cleared of Jews] on the "Aryan" side and to make the ghetto smaller. Hundreds of the newly homeless arrived and had to be squeezed in among the Jews in the already crowded ghetto. There was always a new list of needy poor and several liters of water had to constantly be poured into the kitchen kettles.

T.O.Z. [*Towarzystwo Ochrony Zdrowia* – the Association for the Protection of Health, known as the Jewish Health Organization] played a great part in providing help. This organization, under the leadership of Roziner, a well-known Czenstochower aid worker, tried to obtain permission to arrange several theatrical events in the ghetto, with the help of the *Judenrat*. After many difficulties, the theatrical ventures were finally carried out, which brought in a certain sum of money for the aid fund. Amateurs who once acted in the theater took part in the performance. The homeless *khazan* [cantor] from the Poizner [Poznan] area organized a mixed chorus of former musicians performing solos. The poor children from the orphan house also appeared. A great deal of effort was made that the clothing and equipment for those taking part be pretty. Jews rushed into the theater. Firstly, everyone wanted to contribute to the aid fund and, secondly, the theater in the ghetto was actually an attraction because it was now three years since the ghetto inhabitants had been permitted to visit a movie theater, any theater, to hear a radio. Therefore, the room was overfilled each time a performance took place and each program had to be repeated many times.

p. 127

*　　*

*

On the day of *Weihnachten* [Christmas Eve] in 1941, gendarmes were placed in the streets at all corners of the ghetto. They stopped every Jewish man, woman and child and took off everyone's fur coats and, in general, every coat that had a piece of fur on it. Mounds of furs were quickly collected on every corner of the streets: expensive "Baghdadn," Astrakhans, foxes and other cheaper kinds of furs. Later, this was all taken away in trucks. The Jewish women and children were left standing in the harshest frost without coats, in light clothing. They quickly ran home. The men were also left in light suits, some without hats, if they had fur on them. The fur was the last thing of worth for many people that they had hidden until a dark hour.

Early the next morning announcements were nailed on all of the gates of the ghetto from the *Judenrat* that the German regime had ordered all of the Jews to hand over all of the furs in their possession during the course of the day and that if items of fur were found with a Jew after that period, they would be shot.

p. 128

The announcement caused great confusion. Many Jews sold their expensive furs to the Poles for very small change; it was thought better something than nothing. Others again gave their furs to their Polish acquaintances "to hide" until the bad times were over. However, the greater part of the population was afraid of the threats and presented their furs to the Germans. Two people were chosen in each house to take the furs from every renter and bring them to the *Judenrat*. The large rooms of the *Judenrat* were immediately filled with the sacks of the collected furs and German and Polish police were placed on watch. The things were then taken over to a large hall on the "Aryan" side where all the Jewish furriers whom the *Judenrat* had been required to provide were seated. The Jewish craftsmen worked for months remodeling the furs into various clothing for the German soldiers who were fighting on the Russian front in harsh frosts.

The Germans were very pleased with the work of the Czenstochower Jewish furriers and large transports of Jewish furs arrived from other cities and they were remodeled here.

However, the Jews went around in their light summer clothing. On some clothing, from which the forbidden fur trimmings on the collar and sleeves had been removed, the stiff lining showed through and later a piece of some sort of cloth was sewn on so that in the course of one day there was not one Jew in the ghetto, man, woman or child, with the smallest piece of fur on them. If there was a piece of fur found in the possession of a Jew during the various searches, the owner along with others who knew about it or had any connection were taken away to the cemetery and shot there.

p. 129

At the same time, when there was need and want in the ghetto, a restaurant was organized in the first house near the ghetto border by several tradesmen and gastronomic workers where one could obtain fine, delicious foods, almost as in pre-war times. It was not understood how the owners were able to make such good foods from products that could not be obtained anywhere. The prices were higher and the premises were visited by those Jews who were able to indulge in paying out a large amount of money. Poles, who wished to meet their Jewish acquaintances in order to carry out various business, also began to come in. The Jewish police would enjoy themselves in the nearby little rooms of the premises, but always after eight o'clock in the evening when all of the Jews had to be at home and only they alone had permission to be in the street. There were also other Jews who had night passes – members of the *Judenrat*, several higher officials of the *Judenrat* and other Jewish young people with privileges that no one knew how they had been acquired. All of these people would pay large sums in the new restaurant and the owners had a good business.

In time the premises also became known on the "Aryan side;" one received such meals at the ghetto restaurant that were not even available on the "Aryan side." Polish guests, therefore, also began to come. They sneaked in at night through a back door and ate there and got drunk as in former times.

p. 130

A new coffee house quickly opened opposite the restaurant where one could receive the best-baked goods and the best cakes with good coffee. These premises were very well visited and in time developed regular guests. The gendarmes would come into these Jewish premises from time to time and carried out to their autos roasted geese and hens, other foods and alcohol and wine. The owners were cursed and beaten. The Germans could not understand where the Jews were getting all of the good things. They arrested one of the owners and put him in jail. His partner and good friend succeeded in arranging for his freedom after a few weeks. The restaurant continued to exist after the arrest. The police would also seize Jews for work in these premises. However, this did not scare people and immediately after the people were taken away to work, other guests would arrive at the premises.

p. 130

Chapter XXVI

Traitors

The ghetto oozed a scum of Jewish swindlers and "fixers" who for money would agree to take care of various matters with the regime. They would promise to extract those arrested by the Gestapo and meanwhile drew large sums, ostensibly needed to be used in order to carry out the release. After receiving the money, the "fixer" found a means to extricate himself and he kept the money.

A strange young man named Besser appeared among us. He and his wife opened a small restaurant where this sinister business was carried out.

p. 131

This is how it would be done:

When a Jew who still had some possessions was arrested, a person would appear who would contact the family or wife of the arrestee and in a conversation would "accidentally" mention that there is an honest man named Besser who had already extricated people from the Gestapo and only he could help. Those closest to the arrestee knew that if he were not freed immediately on the first day after the arrest, he would be sent away to Auschwitz, from which there was no return. The unfortunate, therefore, grasped at every hope and thus fell into the hands of the swindler.

Another swindler was active here – one named Szeftel – incidentally, a Czenstochower resident. He was an informer even during the First World War. It was said that he legitimized himself with the Hitlerists with those papers, but this time his activities took on a wider scope. Now he made denunciations in order to then be able to "make things good." In this way, he had twice as good a business with each "transaction."

Jews were not permitted to possess gold, foreign currency and various goods. The main foreign currency office in Krakow organized a control brigade that made lightning visits to the cities where they expected to find something and it controlled the local foreign currency offices at the same time. Szeftel, the informer, had his German acquaintances on this commission and he told them where to storm in for a search.

The searches made on Szeftel's instructions were so thorough that the searchers did not leave the invaded residence until they had found something. The residence was simply turned over: floors were ripped up, the ovens were taken apart, every corner was ransacked dozens of times until something was found. If Szeftel had indicated something – it must be found! The owner of the residence was arrested and tortured for so long that he revealed the names of his partners, who were also arrested. Such a bit of work was recognized as Szeftel's and, therefore, only he could "make it good."

p. 132

The wives and relatives of the arrestees would then run to Szeftel, who was immediately ready to do a favor for the unfortunate people. He would assure them that if he himself could not take care of the matter, he would send his son and if his son also could not help, he would send his daughter. Szeftel's "making it good" would usually end in this way: several people would be freed for the substantial sum that he extracted from the unfortunate ones and the others were deported. Szeftel explained that this could not be otherwise because if the commission members carried out a search, they then had to show that they had found guilty ones.

There was a series of other swindlers who operated as criminals among us in the bitter, dark days. This lasted until one day the Gestapo attacked the swindlers, took a great deal of money, gold and things of value from them. Then they were arrested and sent to Auschwitz. It later became known that the Germans eliminated them because they knew too many secrets and became inconvenient for the Gestapo.

* *

*

A decree was issued by the regime that all non-German residents of the "General-Government" had to report to receive a *kennkarte* [identity card].

The identity card for Poles was of a green color, for Jews and gypsies – yellow. In addition to this, a "J" was found right on the first page of the Jewish *kennkarte*, that is *Jude* [Jew], in order that as soon as one had the document in his hand, it was immediately known with whom one was dealing.

p. 133

Polish officials were employed in the ghetto with the preparation work for issuing the identity cards. They collected the payment and sent the Jews to be photographed. A large penalty was connected with not obeying the order. All Jews, men and women from age 12 on, fell under this law and it was carried out just as every previous law.

* *
*

The German labor office issued a decree that all Jews from 12 to 60 had to appear at the labor office with all of their documents. There everyone was questioned and what he or she had done from childhood on was recorded. Everyone received a piece of paper on which was written that he had been recruited by the Germans for forced labor.

In time the *Judenrat* received an order to renovate premises for a Jewish branch of the German labor office. The premises were renovated and a sign was hung out over it with the words: *Juden Einsatz* [Jewish Employment]. Immediately after this, a demand was made in the ghetto that all of the Jews report to the new office of the *Juden Einsatz*. There, everyone received a work booklet that was called a *meldekarte* [registration card] that was annotated as to where one was employed. The *meldekarte* also served as a document to legitimize oneself.

When the issuing of the *meldekartes* was completed, the German labor office's *Juden Einsatz* branch took the Jewish workers under its supervision.

The leader of the *Juden Einsatz* was a German aged 50 with the name of Frentzel, an absolute drunk. All decrees about Jewish workers were directed to him, and Herr Frentzel had the power to order that Jews be grabbed off the streets for work and, in general, he could cause a great deal of trouble if he wished. The German labor office was entirely under his authority. Therefore, the officials in the Jewish labor office would often treat him to a good drink and in this way made him "one of their own," as one referred to this.

p. 134

On a summer morning in 1942, Jewish policemen woke all of the men in the ghetto and in the name of the German regime ordered them to appear at the large new market. Anyone who hid would be shot. Everyone appeared at the market, where high German officials, the city captain, German leaders of the ammunition factories and the leader of the *Juden Einsatz*, Frentzel, were found and at the side stood officials of the Jewish labor office with papers in their hands. Frentzel called out the names of Jews who were employed in German ammunition factories and in other enterprises. Those whose names were called out were immediately taken to their workplaces. The Jewish officials continually handed Frentzel new lists of names. The purpose of this gathering immediately became clear. The German officials carried out an inspection in order to see if every Jew was employed in work and if Frentzel was carrying out his office appropriately. It turned out that of the 14,000 Jews, only 2,000 were unemployed. It appeared that the inspection turned out well. The 2,000 Jews were led to a factory building that stood empty and a guard of Polish police was placed to watch them. No one knew what awaited these people. Days passed and the people remained under arrest in terrible conditions. They slept on the bare earth, the food they received came only from the *Judenrat* kitchen and no one was permitted to approach them.

p. 135

The *Judenrat* worked on Herr Frentzel to get him to intervene so that the people would be freed; he should state that he needed the men for work. After many days and long efforts, the end came with the payment of several hundreds of thousand *zlotys* for their liberation.

* *

*

The *Judenrat* received an order from the regime to create a *gemeinschaft-werke* [community works], that is, a shop where various workshops would be arranged that would carry out work for the military. For the privilege of arranging such a workshop, the *Judenrat* was required to pay a half million *zlotes* to the treasury of the city administration. The premises of the closed Jewish *Metulurgia* factory was allocated, for which it was necessary to pay the Germans 20,000 *zlotes* a month rent. All Jewish artisans had to submit themselves with their machines to the disposal of the shop.

In order to receive the demanded money, the *Judenrat* opened a registration of people who would work in the shop where work would be done for the German military and where there were the most secure positions. Each Jew wanted to have a document that he was employed and was a useful person. To be worthy of being recorded as officials, tradesmen or workers in the shop, each one had to pay several thousand *zlotes*. People pursued a place in the shop and a saying emerged – "Everyone needs to be covered," that is, have a workplace.

Everyone was seized by panic, everyone wanted to be "covered." Large sums flowed into the *Judenrat*; people sold everything from their home and on their person in order to be "covered" in the shop that was being organized. Everyone who left the *Judenrat* with a note that he was recorded in the shop felt lucky. The registration of the shop workers never ended. The *Judenrat* realized that the registration was a good source of income and there were always fresh people interested in a shop position.

p. 136

Finally, the organizers proceeded to organize the shop. Former owners of factories were chosen as directors of the shop. Former engineers were responsible for individual workshops. Trade engineers were chosen for the offices and warehouses, along with former large entrepreneurs and substantial merchants. These people had to pay large sums in order to receive the highest offices in the shop.

The first activity of the newly organized shop consisted of taking the machines from the artisans. The lesser officials of the shop traveled around with horses and wagons from one artisan to another and mainly from one tailor to another in order to take their sewing machines. Terrible scenes were thus played out; there was fighting between the officials and the artisans. The tailor's sewing machine was his source of income. He lived with it during the course of his entire life as with his right hand; he could not part with it. He knew that being "covered" would still not give him any income. If he worked in the shop the entire day for a little bit of soup from the kitchen, his family would starve together with him.

The *Judenrat* did not have any other choice. It could not take a stand on the side of the Jews. It then existed in order to carry out the German orders and the German orders were aimed at the devastation of Jewish life down to the ground. The tailors from whom the sewing machines had been taken were doubly embittered, because it was a Jew who had taken their machines from them. It was the same in similar cases. The fact that Jewish officials were taking their last possessions at the orders of the Germans caused them special pain. The pain was much stronger than if it had been done by the Germans themselves. We knew that the Germans were our enemy, but that a Jew would rake the fire with their hands for the Germans! However, the sophisticated evil to organize things so that one Jew would take the last possession from another and bring it to the enemy really pierced.

p. 137

The German police coped with the recalcitrant artisans with their rubber sticks; they took the machines and placed them in the shop.

The furrier workshop on the "Aryan" side that remodeled Jewish furs for the military was also transferred to the shop. Other workshops for locksmiths, carpenters and so on were organized there. The shop began its work in the middle of the summer of 1942.

The majority of the people who paid large sums for being accepted in the shop were not really artisans, so the workshops would not have been able to exist only with them. Therefore, the artisans whose machines had been taken away by force were pressured to come to work. They were simply forced to work. A number of non-working people were placed around each artisan. However, the fact was that the thousands of people from whom the *Judenrat* had taken money could not be employed. A system of protection began; wives of the members of the *Judenrat* and others of the privileged sat in the shop near a table ostensibly handing something to the tailors, while the real working women, who had receipts for the sums they had paid, remained outside the shop. The *Judenrat* knew how to calm them with the explanation that it was enough to have a receipt for the paid sum and it was not actually necessary to work in the shop.

p. 138

Many German officials often visited the communal workshop and examined the organization, the people and the work. The workers explained the shop's organization, made efforts to introduce themselves in the best possible way. The Germans winked at everything, good... good... Those employed in the shop were satisfied that the Germans were convinced of their usefulness, as opposed to those who remained outside the shop, envying those who were "covered."

People became frantic and used every means possible to be "covered" because news reached us from other cities about the existence of a *Juden-ausrotung komando* [Jewish extermination commando] that had the task of sending all of the Jews who were not employed to extermination camps.

The Jewish labor office was besieged by men and women. Everyone wanted to obtain work. However, the labor office did not have workplaces to employ so many people. A business of work positions began that was referred to as *placowkes* [Polish word for post or position]. Large sums of money began to be paid for a *placowske* and it reached the point that people were pushed out of jobs, for which they had already paid. Great scandals occurred of deceptions in usurping jobs. Everyone was controlled by one frantic desire: "They must be covered!" They paid large sums of money for *placowkes* in the ammunition factories or for a position as an official in the *Judenrat*. The brigadiers in the Jewish labor office sold *placowkes* and thus earned a great deal of money. The price for *placowkes* constantly rose and for a "broom" the payment reached into the thousands. The work of cleaning the streets was called "a broom." Every morning and evening groups of Jews with brooms in their arms marched to the large city squares and in front of the government offices and cleaned the streets there. This was the easiest work and after great effort this was assigned to the intellectuals. Professors, lawyers, former directors and others marched in rows twice a day under the leadership of a brigadier with their brooms in their arms. Thus they went through the most beautiful streets of the city until they arrived at their workplaces. There they cleaned and gathered the garbage that people, horses, cattle and Germans left after themselves. While marching across the "Aryan streets," they often encountered their former Polish friends and acquaintances. Some would look at them with sympathy; others would openly ridicule them with mockery. However, the "street cleaners" were satisfied because they had a certificate from the city managing committee that they were employed and thus were protected from being sent away who knows where.

p. 139

The first concern for everyone was "to be covered" – that is, covered by obtaining a job somewhere. When acquaintances met, their first question was were they already "covered" and did they work in a *Batrieb A* [Company A], that is, an enterprise that carried out work directly with military purposes, which was considered the most secure means against "transfers."

When I learned that the "transfer" would first of all occur for older people and children, I became very frightened for the fate of my parents and began looking for the means to save them. As my wife was considered the best milliner in the city and made hats for the German women, she told her clients that she could not obtain the materials for the hats in the colors for which they asked. However, there was a way: there was an older man in the city who was a good dyer and if she could obtain this man as her employee, it would be possible to have materials for hats in all colors. Because of his higher age – 71 – it was very difficult to obtain a workplace for my father. But then after continued efforts, we were successful in receiving permission for my wife to have him as an employee as a dyer of materials for hats. I could not obtain such a position for my mother because a woman of 70 could not be employed in a fashion salon. However, I obtained a position for my mother and also for my brother with an administrator of Jewish houses. My brother became a collector and my mother, a guard. All of my acquaintances were envious of me because I was successful in "covering" my family.

p. 140

Chapter XXVII

Harsher Terror

Signs appeared of harsher terror in relation to the Jewish population:

A member of the Gestapo once stopped a Jewish young man outside of the ghetto and took him into a courtyard and there in a corner shot him. The Jewish police received an order by telephone two hours later that they should come with a horse and wagon and take away "*dos dreck* [this dirt]" (that is, the young man) that would be found at the indicated address.

Several days later, after eight o'clock at night, two young men were detained in the ghetto by the Gestapo in a passing car. The Jewish young men presented their night passes, which the Gestapo took from them and ordered them to enter the car. They drove the young men to the cemetery, took everything they had from them and shot them.

Another case happened within a few days that revealed the new, harsher pattern:

p. 141

The Jewish Dr. Wolberg, leader of the sanitary system in the ghetto, was called to the office of the city captain. Having to wait a long time in the corridor, Dr. Wolberg started to read a German newspaper. A representative of the city captain whom the doctor did not know well was passing and tore the newspaper out of his hands in anger. The German then slapped the doctor several times and said that a Jew does not need to read a newspaper, particularly in German.

The *Judenrat* received an order from the regime that it should move out of its house on *Aleja* 11 in two days and set up their offices on Garncarska Street in the house in which the Artisans School had been located for dozens of years and from which all of the machines and all of the tools of the locksmith, carpenter and electrical divisions were removed and given to the Polish Artisans School. The *Judenrat* endeavored to carry out the order in the designated period and to give the house to the regime. Two days later, the neighboring house at *Aleja* 9 was made *Judenrein* [free of Jews] in the usual way. The residents of the houses on the First *Aleja* were afraid that their houses on this street would be made *Judenrein* and they began to transfer whatever they could from their residences to the farthest streets. Others again brought goods and valuables to Polish acquaintances to be hidden. Every day they expected gendarmes to come and drive them from their residences; thus they lived in fear and insecurity.

The panic was even greater when the frightening news from the Warsaw Ghetto arrived at the end of August. Rumors spread that the *Juden Ausrotung Komando* [Jewish Extermination Commando] would be coming to Czenstochow. Many began to arrange secret hiding places in cellars and attics.

p. 142

The *Judenrat* received an order from the city captain without an explanation to make a payment of a contribution in the high amount of 55,000 *zlotys*. It was decided at a meeting of the *Judenrat* that the sum must be paid just as the earlier contribution. Several gave as a reason that if the sum were successfully paid quickly, it would save the Jewish population from the danger that was coming closer to us. However, the question emerged: From where would so much money come so quickly? Taxing a large number of people would take a long time. Therefore, it was decided to demand of the affluent Jews that they immediately lend the *Judenrat* this sum and then when the money was collected from the population, 70 percent of the loaned money would be returned.

The well-to-do Jews in the ghetto were summoned to the *Judenrat*, where the president described the approaching danger that threatened all of the Jews if the sum were not paid during the required term. The greatest number of those assembled immediately gave the required sums and those remaining paid the next morning. Those who had again not fulfilled the demand of the *Judenrat* were placed in a cellar by the police until they paid the set amount.

The money was given to the city captain. It seemed that the chairman had received complements from the city captain because from that day on the *Judenrat* spread the rumor that what happened in Warsaw would not happen here because we fulfilled the demands of the regime. When the *Juden Ausrotung Komando* came to us, the German regime in Czenstochow would explain that the Czenstochower Jews work and fulfill all of their duties as regards the regime and thus the Jewish population would be saved.

p. 143

The *Judenrat* sent demands to everyone who was suspected of still having possessions. A special commission was created, which determined the sum that each had to pay. Most paid and the stubborn ones were again forced to pay by the police. However, the money needs of the *Judenrat* were so large that the newly collected money melted in their hands and the several dozen wealthy people never again saw the money they had loaned to the *Judenrat*.

* *
*

A local man, a well-known Jew in the city, received a letter from his daughter in Berlin through secret means. Years earlier she had married a German who was an important figure in Germany. She was successful in remaining with her husband. She wrote to her parents, who were always the dearest in the world to her, that she knew definitely from unquestionable German sources about the extermination of the Jews in the countries occupied by the Germans. Therefore she advised her parents to commit suicide. She informed them of various chemical means to poison themselves that would not create any pain. She wrote that her parents should do this quickly because time was short.

If she and her son, Heinrich, were destined to live, she would sometimes be able to come to their visit their graves. Only if they committed suicide would she be able to find their graves and if they did not do this, but waited for the general extermination, they would suffer a great deal. If, however, she and her son did not survive the frightening times, and this was entirely possible if it was learned that she is a Jew, her husband would do it [visit their graves] and would also write to her sister, Liza, in Palestine so she would know where to find her parents' graves. She took leave of her parents in the letter with moving words. He son also took leave of his grandparents in a heartfelt manner. Her husband also wrote a warm letter to his in-laws and assured them that he was doing everything possible to keep alive his beloved wife and only son.

p. 144

The paper on which the bizarre and tragic words were written by the daughter to her parents was bent here and there as if swollen. The paper had become wet from the daughter's tears as she wrote the letter and had later dried out. She wrote that she would have preferred to send the tears, wet and hot, straight from her eyes, but she asked them to accept the crushed paper just as she had sent dried flowers in her letters to her parents in the past.

The contents of this letter floated over the ghetto as a specter. It threw terror into everyone who heard of it or read it. Calculations were made of a situation in which a daughter was persuaded to give such advice to her parents. The letter increased fear in people and strengthened the panic.

*   *

*

Early on the morning of Yom Kippur, the 21st of September 1942, the streets of the ghetto looked like every other day. The work groups went to their workplaces; the Jewish women did not go to prayer, but to wash the floors, windows and doors of the various German offices; the teachers, lawyers and all other intellectuals marched to their workplaces in rows with brooms on their shoulders. All the other Jews, who had somewhere to work, quickly ran through the streets, tapping out a slave-cadence with their wooden shoes.

Here and there people moved along the wall, as if avoiding being noticed too much. These were older people going to the synagogue in order to remain there the entire day for prayer.

Notice about the death penalty for Jews for leaving the ghetto in German and Polish

p. 145

The officials sat in the offices of the *Judenrat* without any work; today they had not received any interested clients. One official was carrying on a conversation with the German chief, Herr Frentzel. He told him about the fear that reigned among the Jews, that "deportations" would take place. Frentzel was angered and said, "Your side has become crazy, *es komt nichts for* [it will not happen]." At the request of the official, Frentzel telephoned several places and was assured that nothing would happen, because where would he find the thousands of people who he needed to work?

However, the mood in the ghetto was anxious. Some knew and said that in the morning, on the 22nd of September, a *Juden auszilding* [deportation of Jews] would take place here in Czenstochow. News came from the "Aryan side" that there were already Latvians and Ukrainians in the city, who had boasted somewhere that they had come here to make an end of the Jews. A Polish woman, the owner of a restaurant, said that Ukrainians and Latvians, who had arrived the day before from Warsaw, were being fed in her restaurant. They had told her that they were in the ghetto there for two months to liquidate the ghetto. Now they would do the same thing to the Czenstochower Jews.

The news was carried through the ghetto like a windstorm and the terror grew from minute to minute.

All of the known non-commissioned gendarme officers, who had received nicknames for their cruelty, were seen assembled on the large square near the boundary of the ghetto; "the white head," "the little belt," "the murderer," "the throat" and still others. They stood there with their bicycles and held discussions. They talked and talked. It lasted an hour; one rode away and then came back with still another one. Then one again went away and came back. They carried on their conversation quietly; they pointed with their hands here to one street, there to another. It gave the impression that something was being planned here. One Jew showed this to another Jew and the panic grew.

p. 146

In the late afternoon hours, a calming message from the chairman of the *Judenrat* was spread that he had received an order from the regime that he should calm the Jews, [by saying] that nothing would happen and the gossip was groundless.

At the same time, an officer from the gendarmerie and his wife came to the artisans and ordered things for themselves, the production of which would take two weeks. This was a silent notice to the artisans that according to what was being said that if something happened tomorrow morning it would make the carrying out of the order uncertain. The officer laughed at this and gave assurances that nothing would happen to us in the city.

The good news was immediately spread lightening fast through the ghetto.

The fear again fell from the faces of the people and they again breathed easier.

p. 146

Chapter XXVIII

The *Aktsia* of the 22nd of September 1942

The assurances from the *Judenrat*, from the regime and from all other sources could not calm all of the Jews. The bad signs, warning of the opposite, were too clear.

p. 147

Therefore, many people did not sleep after the end of Yom Kippur, but kept a vigil in their residences. It was a very dark night. As usual, the streetlights were turned off because of *luft-schutz* [anti-aircraft defense]. However, those who were awake were amazed at suddenly seeing through their windows that all of the electrical lights were suddenly so brightly illuminated, just as before the war. Suddenly, anti-aircraft defense became unimportant. A fitter from the electrical institution driving through the streets in the ghetto was in control of the management of the lights.

I went out onto the balcony of my residence, from which all of the *Aleja* could be seen far into the new market. I saw divisions of military formations, short, thick people, dressed in very long coats with guns in their arms, previously unnoticed by us. In addition to them, there were gendarmes. They marched into the ghetto in groups, stopping at each house gate and leaving one or two of their men and in this way placed guards. Under my balcony, at the boundary of the ghetto, two gendarmes with helmets on their heads remained standing. A little farther, on the "Aryan" side, stood two others. In the middle of the *Aleja* patrols of gendarmes and Ukrainians marched back and forth. In the quiet of the night, various military commands were heard from afar:

"Right, left, march!"

Someone stopped in front of our gate and called to the guard to open it. No one in the residences was sleeping. We turned our gaze to the gate; it appeared that a Polish policeman came to call the Jewish police aides and several policemen who lived in the house to immediately report to the precincts. We did not get any answers to our questions about what was happening. He was edgy and left immediately to call other Jewish policemen from other houses.

p. 148

We heard shooting and shouting by Germans at around five o'clock in the morning. The shooting and curses lasted until the day began and, suddenly, we saw that large masses of Jews with small packages on their backs were being forced to the square by the Germans, where the previous night the gendarmes had held their discussions. We, the residents of the artisan's house, were enveloped in fear. We gathered together, several families in one residence, and from time to time secretly looked out through the windows. We saw the way in which the Gestapo with the *totenkop* [skull] markings on their hats and uniforms, with revolvers in their hands, were constantly forcing new multitudes of Jews to the square.

The *aktsia* accompanied with shooting and curses lasted for several hours. Then we saw a Jewish policeman enter our house. Last night he had left his wife here with relatives. Several of us ran down to him to the residence that he had entered. We saw him standing and crying like a small child. He told us that horrible things were happening in the ghetto: when the Jewish policemen arrived at the precinct early in the morning they received an order from Degenhardt, the chief of the gendarmes, who was leading the entire *aktsia*, to carry it out exactly according to the instructions they had received. Whoever did not obey the order would be shot on the spot. The first task received by the Jewish police was to enter all of the Jewish residences in the streets they would be shown and tell all of the Jews, men, women and children that they should come out in groups and go to the new market in rows one behind the other. They were only permitted to take along small packages. The residences had to remain open with the keys in the door. Whoever hid would be shot.

p. 149

The chief's order shook the hearts of the Jewish policemen and their faces became pale; they sensed the sorrowful role they had to carry out, but they went to carry out their task. However, it seemed that this was not completely left to the Jewish policemen. The ghetto streets were full of gendarmes and men from the Gestapo who entered the residences and drove out the people, searched everyone's pockets and yelled: "Give money, diamonds!" And took everything of value.

The old and the sick, who could not move, were shot on the spot. This was the shooting that we heard from early morning on.

The policeman told us that he led his mother out of the house because her feet were disabled and she could not move by herself. But as he led her through the streets, someone seized him from behind and threw him to the ground. He got up on his feet quickly and saw a murderer with a revolver in his hand pointed at his mother. He only had time to shout out: "This is my mother!" And three shots echoed, his mother fell down and quickly breathed out her soul. He carried her into a courtyard and hid her in a garden, covering her with branches. The policeman burst into tears and left.

The Jewish policemen, who lived with us in the artisan's house, arrived at around three o'clock in the afternoon. They looked tired and broken. Later, when they had calmed down a little, they began to tell us what had happened in the ghetto.

One explained how small, beautiful children from three to eight, who had been given to Poles on the "Aryan side" a day earlier, because of fear of the *aktsia* and for whom great sums were paid so that they would be hidden, were forced back by the Poles. The children ran around frightened and confused, but the Germans and Ukrainians did not allow them to go back into the ghetto, but chased them to the square, where masses of people were forced together. The children cried and screamed, but no one looked at them. The masses of thousands of people were chased by the German and Ukrainian murderers with sticks and revolvers, so that the children were simply crushed and trampled under the feet of those being chased.

p. 150

The *aktsia* involved the streets: Garibaldi, Wilson, Krutke, Kawje and part of Warsawer Street. It was decided that 7,000 Jews should be gathered and deported during the first *aktsia*.

Degenhardt, the chief, stood in the market with a small stick in his hand like an orchestra conductor and watched the passing multitudes. When he noticed a healthy young man or a beautiful young woman, he pointed with the stick and immediately, the person pointed out was taken from the row and placed at the side. This meant – remains. Those saved had to leave those closest to them. This had to happen very quickly. There was no leave taking here. Tears ran over cheeks, but everything happened quickly, quickly. The murderers kept "order," pushing and pulling and shouting with wild voices: Quickly, quickly!

The chief ordered the Jewish doctors and their families to be placed in quarantine and that they remain there. He also said that the wives and children of the Jewish policemen should also be taken there. The unmarried doctors and policemen looked for those closest to them or female acquaintances and they were taken into quarantine as their wives, in this manner saving them from being deported.

p. 151

The large mass of people was led to the coal train station, Warta, where gendarmes were waiting in railway cars. An order was given that "all Jews should take their shoes off their feet and lay them on a side." Immediately mountains of shoes, each pair tied together with its shoelaces, grew. Then came the order: "Enter the railway cars." Pushing, congestion and confusion began. The railway cars were greatly overcrowded; there were more than 100 people pushed into each railway car. The gendarmes and members of the Gestapo also created a tumult in the railway cars. They searched for those better dressed and took whatever they found from them.

The chairman of the *Judenrat* endeavored even harder to have his wife brought to the office of the *Judenrat* and in this way to save her. But, when he went to bring her there, he learned from the Jewish policemen that she had already been loaded into a railway car. He ran to the gendarme officer, who knew him and asked him to help him extract his wife, citing the permission he had received from the chief, Degenhardt. The officer took him to the railway car and freed his wife. When she left the railway car, a former neighbor tossed a small child into her arms and she brought it with her. Everyone struck out their hands to the chairman pleading – "Take me with you – I am weak – My heart will not last in the over-packed railway car." However, the wide railway car doors on small wheels were closed by the gendarme and at once the pleas were silenced. All of the other railway cars were also closed and the train moved from the spot.

p. 152

The several dozen people whom the chief had ordered to be left were taken to the shop.

The electric lights that had burned for the entire day in all of the streets in honor of the great holiday of driving the Jews out were shut off. The wagons with the 7,000 pairs of shoes were driven away from the railway cars to the German warehouses and Degenhardt, the chief, was informed that the *aktsia* had ended.

*   *

*

When those in the ghetto learned that those rescued had been taken to the premises of the shop, everyone searched for a means to enter it.

Jews hacked through bricks and cut through fences quietly during the night and created exits to Krutke Street in the houses of the ghetto that bordered on Krutke Street, where the shop was located. There they bribed the Polish policemen who watched the shop in which the Jews were located. If the policemen were honest people, they would allow the Jews in for money and, if not – they shot them at the entrance to the shop. Therefore, the road to the shop was bound with great risk.

After the *aktsia* the streets of the ghetto were guarded by day and by night and the gates of the houses were locked. Often, the Jews behind the closed gates beckoned the passing Jewish policemen and asked that they take them to the shop in order to be rescued from deportations. But the policemen did not have the right to do so. In addition, there was not a large number of Jews in the shop and when new ones were brought there, the policemen who were guarding the shop would have noticed it immediately.

The Jews locked in the ghetto knew that in the German housing office, where the large warehouses of Jewish furniture were found, the Jewish workers were not permitted to go home after work during the day of the *aktsia*. It was interpreted that the head of the housing office wanted to protect his workers from deportation. Therefore, people had hacked through walls, climbed over garden fences in order to enter there. Those who after so much hardship arrived there had to hide from the German head. Men, women and children lay on the bare earth and agreed to everything in order to save themselves from deportation.

p. 153

The Jewish policemen secretly explained that three days after the first *aktsia*, on the 25th of September, the second *aktsia* would take place, when the trains that had taken the Jews away would come back empty. They also revealed that of the local leaders of the regime, only one had command over the Jews – the chief, Degenhardt. The city chief demanded his Jews for necessary work, but the chief did not permit this. The ammunition factory wanted their Jewish workers to remain; the chief refused. The Gestapo also did not receive any Jews for work. The chief was the only leader and commander over the Jews.

The artisan's house on *Aleja* number 14 was also closed and guarded just as all of the houses in the ghetto. The artisans in the house walked around saddened over the fate of those closest to them in the ghetto and also worried about their own fate. None of the Germans who they knew who had earlier consoled and assured them that nothing would happen appeared after the *aktsia*. None of their clients, German or Polish, were allowed into the house. However, we knew that they came to the house and told the gendarmes who stood guard that the handworkers had materials that they wanted to take before the Jews were sent away, but no one was let in to us. Through the window, we saw clients moving around in front of the house.

p. 154

The nights were dark, but the ghetto was brightly lit. Shooting was heard and we knew that each shot meant that a Jew had fallen while going through the street, at the opening of a gate, while climbing over a fence somewhere and so on. No one in the ghetto slept; no one took off their clothing to go to sleep. Food began to be scarce. One helped the other. In general, one was unable to eat because of an aching heart. This lasted until Friday, the 25th of September.

p. 154

Chapter XXIX

The Second *Aktsia*

A day before the second *aktsia,* the Jewish policemen received an order to appear at the Jewish commissariat the next morning at four o'clock.

The second *aktsia* was carried out exactly as the first. The Jewish policemen entered the residences, giving the Jews the news that they must appear with their small packages at the gates of their houses. Then the gendarmes, Ukrainians and Polish policemen arrived and drove them out of the gates to the market.

Just as the first time, old people and the sick were shot on the spot because they could not walk as fast as the murderers wanted.

A "selection" took place at the market just as during the first *aktsia.* The captain pointed with his small stick to vigorous men and young women, whom he said should be left in order to send them to slave labor later. Very often, the healthy looking men were asked their occupation. Locksmiths, cabinetmakers and electricians were quickly driven to the other side to remain. And again tragic scenes were played out during their separation from those close to them.

p. 155

As earlier, the small number of those "chosen" for slave labor were taken to the shop and the thousands of those sentenced to be deported were driven like cattle so they could be loaded in the train wagons.

p. 155

Chapter XXX

Hunger in the Ghetto

After the second *aktsia* 25,000 Jews remained in the ghetto who waited for their uncertain fate.

The hunger became sharper. The poor population that lived from their daily earnings and did not have any reserves did not have anything to eat on the day after the *aktsia*.

The food products from all of the residents of a number of houses were gathered together and cooked in a common kettle. The wealthier who did not agree to cooperate were forced to do so by the poor.

We in the craftsmen's house that bordered on other houses in the ghetto noticed through a window that the Jews in those houses were showing through signs that they were suffering from hunger. The craftsmen immediately began to organize all the help that was possible.

There was also a lack of food in the craftsmen's house; this house was really ragged, but several poor, Polish women lived in the house who understood how to take advantage of the situation and they bought food products on the "Aryan" side that they brought into the house little by little and then sold at higher prices. Each artisan bought food from these women and threw part of it over to the neighboring house where the Jews suffered from hunger. The artisans expanded their support and ordered that the food be thrown over from the nearby house to the house farther in the ghetto.

p. 156

The Jewish policemen, who lived in the craftsmen's house also bought bread and other food products and brought them to the ghetto and to the quarantine facilities or to the shop and saved those closest to them from hunger.

Other Jewish policemen in the ghetto also came to the craftsmen's house and bought food products and then sold them in the ghetto for a higher price.

All of this only alleviated the needs a little for a few individuals, but not for the 25,000 souls.

*   *   *

Just as after the first *aktsia*, every means was used after the second *aktsia* in the ghetto to enter the shop in order to be saved. Degenhardt, the chief, understood how to use this in order to extort the last items held by the Jews anywhere in the ghetto. He informed the president of the *Judenrat* that if there were ghetto Jews who possessed money or things of value, they could enter the shop in exchange for their remaining possessions. The president received permission from the chief to take the things of value from the Jews, to jot them down with the names of the person giving them. This news spread immediately behind the closed doors of the ghetto houses and everyone who owned something was ready to give away their last possessions in order to save themselves. The president took three of his friends to help and all of them left for the ghetto, each separately accompanied by a Polish policeman. The chief also had several people in the Jewish police to whom he gave the same task. The policemen visited the Jewish houses in the ghetto, even the poorest and took what they had from each one. They gave receipts for the things taken with assurances that the people would be taken to the shop. The chief would drive up with his automobile to the ghetto houses and take the gathered gold and objects.

p. 157

The Gestapo, hearing that Jews were giving money and things of value, also began carrying out the same pursuit. They also found someone in the Jewish police who carried on the "business."

Later, more Jewish policemen took to the same "business" and joined with the gendarmes, with whom they carried out the pursuit in partnership. The Jewish policemen carried out transactions with the Jews and the gendarmes brought the people into the shop. The transfer from the ghetto to the shop was linked to great risk; the gendarmes were often stopped by a non-commissioned officer or officer. In such cases, the gendarmes declared that they were bringing Jews to clear the dead or they chose other pretexts. But cases would occur where a gendarme leading one or two Jews would meet a non-commissioned officer who made assumptions about what was happening. He would then take out his revolver and shoot the Jews in the middle of the street. The gendarme who was leading the Jew usually did not make any great fuss. The money or valuable objects had already been taken by the gendarme. At the most, he got even with the gendarme who had shot "his" Jews when he met the other one leading Jews; he then shot "the others" Jews. Then they made up over a bottle of shnapps and remained friends.

p. 158

Several Jewish factories were located on the same street on which the shop was located, managed by a "trustee," where the owners were employed as tradesmen. Jews hid there on the day before the *aktsia*, hoping that the turmoil would not last long and they would then be able to leave their hiding places "when it became quiet." In the places where no one knew about those hiding, the Jews were protected as opposed to where the "trustee" learned about it and he reported it to the gendarmerie and the Jews were shot on the spot or in the best cases were taken to Katedralne Street, where the Jewish communal kitchen was earlier located and there placed under arrest under heavy police guard until the next *aktsia* during which they would then be deported.

There was a Polish "trustee" in the metal factory of the Itskowicz and Guterman firm named Tiszewski, who posed as a former Polish *Sejm* delegate. He did very well in his business dealings with the owners and had good relations with them. However, when he learned that they were in the factory during the *aktsia*, he drove them out of there and warned his Polish employees and workers that Poles who hid Jews during the war would stand trial for disrupting the solution to the Jewish question in Poland.

The owners were surprised by Czeszewski's* brutality. This person was driven from Poznan by the Germans and arrived in Czenstochow a poor man who did not have the means to live through the day. He became rich with them; he was their "best friend" for three years and he had removed his mask and shown his true nature.

*[Translator's note: The name of the Polish "trustee" is spelled differently in the two paragraphs above.]

p. 159

The owners barely had time to leave the factory and they entered the train wagons barefooted with the first deportees in order not to be shot in the middle of the street.

Czeszewski remained alone in the Jewish factory as the manager, believing that he himself could lead the enterprise. However, he quickly received payment for his meanness: after a short time managing the factory, he was arrested and deported to Auschwitz.

There were two Jewish factories on the same street, Horowicz and Komp's metal factory and the spoon factory of the Landau brothers. A German who had earlier lived in Poland was the "trustee" of both factories. This German helped the Jews to hide and they survived the difficult days of the *aktsias* in safety.

p. 159

Chapter XXXI

Bunkers

There were Jews in the ghetto who created bunkers in attics and cellars and in all possible places. More people knew about a large number of bunkers. Five, 10, 20, 50 people and up to 100 men, women and children were hidden in them. They provided themselves with food products for several days, thinking that the "bad times" would pass and then they could return to their residences. No one expected that after the Jews had been driven out of their homes, police or Germans would guard the residences. The fate of the Jews in the bunkers was a very sad one.

p. 160

Jewish policemen also were not allowed to approach the streets from which the Jews had been driven out. Only Ukrainians and gendarmes stood there and protected the residences from robbery and anyone they met there was shot on the spot. Therefore, the Jews could not emerge from their hiding places. They had no more food; they were without air and the people had to be naked because it was so hot in the holes. Small children were strangled by their mothers because their crying was so terrible. If the mother did not want to do this, others who were in the bunkers did it. No one knew what was happening in the street. They only perceived a silence, but from time to time the heavy steps of military boots were heard and if a number of Jews left the bunkers at night to see what was happening in their residences, they only saw that the houses had been plundered and there was a heavy guard of people with guns, so there was no possibility of leaving the hiding places. They went back into the holes and again remained without food and without air until the next night; then they again crawled out and this was repeated again for several days. The relatives of these hidden people, who were in farther ghetto streets from which the Jews had not yet been driven out, were afraid that the people in the holes would die of hunger because they already knew that the *aktsia* would last a long time. Therefore, they told the Jewish policemen about the secret places and who was there. For large sums of money the policemen helped move the Jews from the bunkers to a house where Jews were located who had not yet been affected by the *aktsia*. The policemen left for the bunkers with their gendarme acquaintances and called into the holes: "Jews, we have come to save you!" They alluded to their relatives, who had sent them here and the hopeless people emerged one by one from their pits and holes. They shook from fear, looking terrible, unwashed, unshaven, and hungry; they could barely stand on their feet. They were led to the farther ghetto street by the gendarmes.

p. 161

Leading the Jews through the streets was very dangerous. If they were stopped by someone along the way, the gendarme who led them had to say that they had been in hiding and he had found them accidentally. Then their lives were dependent on who had stopped them. They could be shot on the spot or sent where there were other Jews waiting to be sent with the next transport. But first they were ordered to give up their money, gold and other things of value. Understandably, at such a dangerous time, no one thought about hiding their money and they surrendered everything.

The Jews from the not yet "cleansed" streets welcomed their guests with whatever they could during these days of hunger. Others newly arrived were envious of the Jews in the locked houses in that they did not have to suffer as much as those in the hiding places and holes, from which not all emerged alive. Many children remained there [i.e. died in the hiding places] and not all of the old people came out of the bunkers.

However, the newly arrived quickly found that there was no one to envy. They learned that everyone expected to be driven into the train wagons the day after to tomorrow. The newly arrived were advised to get enough sleep and to strengthen themselves with whatever was available in order to be able to go with everyone and not be left behind, in order not to be shot on the way by the murderers.

p. 162

Officers from the gendarmerie attacked the commissariat of the Jewish police and searched for Jewish policemen. The money and things of worth that were found on them was taken. In addition they were badly beaten. It appears that the Germans learned of the business that the Jewish policemen had been lately carrying out. It was decreed that a Jewish policeman must not go in the street alone, but with a Polish policeman or with a gendarme. Thus ended their "golden business" to which they had taken so eagerly. Three Jewish policemen (Parosol, Rubinsztajn and Rozenberg) received special passes from the chief to be able to go into the ghetto streets alone. They had a special merit with the chief.

*   *
*

The chief sent a gendarme to the artisans' house for his tailor, Josef Gryn. Several hours later the tailor returned alone, but no longer as a tailor, but wearing a hat of the Jewish police. Gryn became a policeman and he received a pass that gave him the right to enter the ghetto streets.

The artisans related to the new policeman with reserve, but they wanted to know what the chief had told him about conditions in general and about the situation of the artisans in particular. However, the tailors did not want to speak to him too much and nothing was learned from him.

Inspector Linderman appeared at the artisans' house several days after the *aktsia*. He went to the tailor Kac and all of the artisans immediately entered. Finally a German from the city authorities who until then had the artisans under his control appeared. Everyone wanted to know if they were still "his" artisans, whom he and all of his people had made good use of until then. He explained that consultations had occurred between the city chief and Chief Degenhardt about the artisans' house and there was hope that the house would remain under the protection of the city chief and in that case nothing would change in the artisans' house. He would know about it very soon. And he asked that it meanwhile be kept a secret. Everyone surrounded him as someone they knew and he expressed his concern at driving out the Jews.

p. 163

The artisans had strangers living with them who had come into the house during the last few days through walls and fences. They did not appear on the city chief's lists that hung on the walls of the workshops as employed tradesmen. The artisans asked the inspector to add the people to the lists. Inspector Linderman promised that he would come the next day with the city chief's stamp with which he was authorized to place his signature and he would make the arrangements for this in such a way that all of the people who were then in the house would be legalized. However, he warned that no more new people should be allowed to enter because the more Jews who were found in the artisans' house, the more difficult it would be to take care of the matter with Chief Degenhardt.

The artisans were a little excited after the inspector's visit. The hope that they and those closest to them could be saved elevated their mood a little. They warned each other that they should not bring in any strangers. However, someone then arrived who had taken a chance with his life, scrambling by night over fences and walls in order to crawl into the artisans' house – no one could refuse entry to this unfortunate person.

p. 164

Inspector Linderman came in the morning with an official from the
city authorities and started to put together a list of every person who
was found in the artisans' house with each individual artisan.
Linderman taught the artisans how to defend the newly arrived people
to the new official – that they are needed for work. A list was put
together on which 187 souls appeared.

The two Germans declared that the artisans' house remained
under the management of the city chief and the artisans would
continue to be employed there.

The list was closed. Each artisan received a note on which was
enumerated his family and his worker-journeymen. Each note was
signed by Inspector Linderman under the stamp of the city authorities.
This important paper was hung on the most prominent spot of each
workshop and the artisans believed that the "extermination
commando" would not have any power over them.

                            *   *

                                *

Chief Degenhardt appeared in the ghetto on the afternoon of
Sunday, the 27th of September 1942.

Jewish policemen carried baskets with half-kilo breads. The Jews
were led out of each house separately and every one, old and young,
received a half-kilo of bread. The chief stood by at the division of the
bread and speared everyone with his look. He asked some people their
names, with what they were employed; he only looked at others and
gave an angry grumble like a dog. Each one took his little bit of bread
and want back into his house.

We in the artisans' house were curious if we would be called to get
bread. Not because we were waiting for a piece of bread. Everyone in
the artisans' house could buy bread and there was enough money for
this, but it was rather that if the artisans were still under the
authority of the city chief and not Chief Degenhardt, we did not need
to receive any bread. Therefore, we were surprised when Jewish
policemen began to call us, saying that we should go down to the
courtyard, stand in rows and go out to the street for bread. This
signified that we were considered just as the other Jews from all of the
other houses that were waiting to be sent away.

p. 165

However, there was no time to think this through. All obediently went out into the street. Chief Degenhardt looked at the artisans and their children and "journeymen" very carefully. Each one of us was given a portion of bread and we were taken back into the house.

Meanwhile the Jewish policemen who lived with us in the artisans' house returned from their work and explained that tomorrow before dawn another *aktsia* would take place that would again involve thousands of Jews.

p. 165

Chapter XXXII

The Third *Aktsia*

The third *aktsia*, which was carried out in the same way as the two earlier ones, took place on the 28th of September 1942.

The residents of several ghetto streets were led out to the market where Chief Degenhardt, surrounded by his accomplices, made a selection of young people and tradesmen who were left and thus separated from their families. The well-known heart rending scenes occurred, as during the earlier *aktsias*, as several thousand Jews were loaded into the cattle cars.

p. 166

After the third *aktsia*, Chief Degenhardt visited the "housing office" on Wilson Street that was under the control of Inspector Linderman. He asked the Jews who were employed there to stand in rows. There was a panic. The Jews, who were hiding there in the attics and closets, shook with fear. Inspector Linderman showed Chief Degenhardt his Jewish workers who were employed there and declared that the "housing office" belonged to the city authorities. At this, Chief Degenhardt answered that the time when the Jews belonged to the city chief and to the Gestapo had passed. Now all of the Jews belonged only to him. Then he placed his small crop in front of Inspector Linderman's nose and left.

It was easy to foresee the consequences of this incident. We knew that each conflict about the Jews between the Germans ended badly for the Jews. The Jews in the "housing office" felt the same way - that their situation had changed for the worst.

Learning of the incident in the "housing office," the artisans of *Aleja* number 14 also realized that their position was very shaky under Linderman's "protection," despite all of his assurances.

* *

*

Mrs. Maszewicz, the actual director of the workshops, appeared at the artisans' house. The artisans wanted to learn about the situation from her. She provided the best of hopes and said that the city chief was applying all means so that the artisans' house would remain the way it was until now and that she was sure that nothing bad would happen here. She again gave out orders to artisans from German clients and said that all of the artisans should continue to work and to help each other in their work in order for the artisans' house to remain active.

p. 167

The artisans again began to work. However, other clients appeared. Instead of the earlier German civilians, in whose hands the fate of the Jews lay, now members of the Gestapo and gendarmes appeared with their wives and children. The artisans would use their so-called "privileged" situation in order to learn something from the new "customers" about the future fate of the artisans. The new clients gave everyone the best hopes. In general, they acted very "decently" in the artisans' workshops, much unlike their attitude in the street when chasing Jews. But it should be understood that this was to make better use of the artisans and that the turn of the artisans had not yet come.

*   *
*

Chief Degenhardt learned that Jews were hiding in bunkers, in attics and cellars and he declared an "amnesty" for all who would come out of their hiding places by themselves by a certain deadline and they would be able to return to their houses.

Jewish policemen accompanied by gendarmes and Ukrainians went into all of the courtyards and shouted: "Jews, We have come to save you from death! Come out from your holes and nothing will happen!"

Many emerged from their hiding places. They were in terrible condition. Starving, faint and neglected. They had surrendered everything that they had of value. Then they were allowed into their houses, which had not yet gone through the *aktsias*.

p. 168

However, there were also others who had good bunkers and food that would suffice for several weeks. These did not listen to the beautiful words of the Jewish policemen and remained in the hiding places.

When the period of the "amnesty" passed, the gendarmes began to energetically search for those hiding. The Jewish policemen, who had their gendarme acquaintances with whom they would carry out various businesses in partnership, went through the courtyards with the gendarmes and searched for the bunkers of Jews. They shouted in Yiddish that if those hidden would emerge by themselves, they would still be saved. They shouted into cellars and up to attics, until they reached people who were already tired of lying in the hiding places and they came out. When the people were outside, they were first asked to surrender everything they possessed. The Jewish policemen were apparently comforting. They would try to persuade the gendarmes to spare their lives, if they surrendered everything. When they had everything of the victims, the gendarmes shot them on the spot. The Jewish policemen would receive a certain percent of the stolen items.

p. 168

Chapter XXXIII

The Subsequent *Aktsias*

The fourth *aktsia*, which played out like the earlier ones, took place on the 1st of October 1942. The *aktsia* also included all of the Jews who were found in the "housing office," which ostensibly remained under the support of the city chief. Degenhardt, the chief [of the gendarmes], ordered to be driven out from there onto the market, not only those who had secretly entered by climbing over walls and fences, but also the tradesmen. Chief Degenhardt did this to spite the city chief.

p. 169

A "selection" was made at the fourth *aktsia* as during the earlier ones and about 700 young boys and girls were left who were later sent away for various kinds of slave labor. The city managing committee received an allocation of a number of those "selected ones" for highway work to pave the streets with cobblestones. Others were sent to the "Hasag" [Hugo Schneider Metallwarenfabrik AG] firm's ammunition factory. There they were first completely undressed and everything of value was taken from them. Then they were taken to a room with a stone floor. This is the place where they were to sleep, but there was not even a little straw to place under themselves. They had to work in this factory for 12 hours a day and they received a piece of bread with a little soup to eat. If anyone succeeded in escaping from there, his two neighbors, that is, those who slept next to him on the stone floor, were shot. The unlucky slaves were beaten for the least thing by the *Folks-Deutschn* [ethnic Germans, living outside Germany] until bloody.

A third group was sent to the "Rakow" iron-glassworks that also belonged to Hasag, the same firm and where there were the same conditions as in the ammunition factory.

*   *

*

One morning the tailor Gryn reported to the artisans of *Aleja* number 14 that Chief Degenhardt would visit all workshops in the artisans' house. All the men and women who were in the artisans' house were placed with the tailors, shoemakers, corset makers, hat makers and linen sewers and so on. They received needles and thread or irons or other tools and they diligently applied themselves to the work. All workshops were active, everything worked, good or bad – that was not important. The main thing was that no one moves around idly without work.

p. 170

The master craftsmen pinned a red order ticket on every piece of work with the name of the German client. Suits, fur coats, military clothing were hung up in the tailor workshops; boots and women's shoes were arranged at the shoemakers, all fastened with the red order tickets. Blouses and dresses hung on special hangers at the tailors of women's clothing, adorned with the red tickets; it was the same in all of the other workshops: at the milliners, underwear seamstresses and so on. All the assistants of the craftsmen were dressed in their aprons, the master craftsmen in their best suits and all efforts were made for the guest who had already sent away 80 percent of the Jews in our city in cattle cars.

Finally, an auto drove up to the artisans' house, from which Degenhardt emerged. Accompanied by Onkelsbach, his devoted driver, he went up to Josef Gryn, the former tailor and present policeman, who began to lead the two Germans through the artisans' workshops. His first visit was to Kac, the tailor of women's clothing, and he examined the beautiful fur coats and coats. He read out the names on the order tickets and recognizing that these were women whose husbands were employed in the office of the city chief, he made ironic and caustic comments at their expense. Then he went to Einhorn, the men's clothing tailor, and with the look of a policeman, he observed the women and men sitting at the sewing machines or with needles and thread in their hands. Seeing the tailor's 13-year old son with a needle and a piece of work in his hand, he asked: "What is this Jewish *drek* [filth, excrement] making?"

p. 171

The tailor, confused, answered that this was his son, an apprentice. In this way he went from workshop to workshop, piercing everything and everyone with police eyes and throwing ironic comments and vicious jokes everywhere. At the milliners he took a light woman's hat weighing several grams in his fat paws and tried to blow it away. The chief also looked at the artistic pieces of the old Fajgenblat and he was shown antiques that this workshop, which had 50 years of existence behind it, had produced. He also was told that the most expensive *poroykhes* [the curtains covering the ark holding the Torah scrolls], which the chief had taken from the *shul* [synagogue] before it was burned and sent to Berlin, were also the work of the old Fajgenblat.

However, the chief was not impressed by anything. He showed scorn and cynicism to everything and everyone. And he left after looking at all of the workshops.

The chief's visit left an anxiety in everyone's heart.

The Polish director of the Jewish police received a decree from Chief Degenhardt that he should put together a list of 50 Jewish policemen who would remain in their posts and the rest, numbering about 200, would be sent away with all of the other Jews during the next transport.

There was a panic among the Jewish policemen. Each one ran to the Polish director and to the Jewish aid director in order to obtain the privilege of remaining among the 50 who would be left. One tried to out do the other with large sums of money in order to save themselves from being sent away barefoot in a cattle car.

p. 172

The Polish director of the Jewish police put together a list of 50 names – it should be understood that in putting together the list, the director took into account the sums of money that he could expect to receive from each one

However, when the chief saw the list, his policeman's nose got a whiff of what was hidden behind everything and he ordered all of the policemen to line up in rows with their wives and children. Then, he himself chose 50 and he ordered the rest to take off their boots and their police hats with the bands, said that they, their wives and children should be taken to the devastated synagogue at the old market under heavy guard where they would remain until the next *aktsia*.

A number of these men sent letters from their detention to their former colleagues who remained in office and threatened to reveal secrets if they did not arrange for their release, but their colleagues were not afraid and left their work colleagues without an answer.

Therefore, nothing else remained for them except to sit in the synagogue and wait for their bitter fate just as the other Jews who through them had been chased and beaten in the course of three years under Degenhardt's regime.

It was learned on the 4th of October 1942 that the Jewish policemen, those remaining, were ordered to take part in the *aktsia* that would take place the next day at daybreak – the fifth *aktsia*.

The fifth *aktsia* began like the earlier ones, but it was noticed immediately that a special plan had been prepared for it. First of all, it took place at a faster pace than all of the earlier ones. At daybreak, earlier than before, the Jews were driven to the new market. This time more Jews were shot in the streets than in the earlier *aktsias*. The chief directed more energetically and with his little stick, and the sticks and twisted straps fell on the Jewish heads more often. The assistants did not permit anyone to run up to the chief to ask for mercy. The train wagons were filled earlier than during the earlier *aktsias* and a thousand pairs of shoes grew more quickly into a mountain. At the end of the march of the thousand Jews to the train wagons, Degenhardt ordered his driver to take him and his closest co-workers to the ghetto. First of all, he visited the collection camp on Katedralna Street and said that all of the Jews there should be driven to the train wagons. After this he ordered that the Jewish policemen be brought there with their wives and children, who were being held under arrest in the synagogue.

p. 173

At the end, the chief and his servants left for the Jewish hospital with his aides and he had the doctors and nurses, who had remained at their posts through all of the previous *aktsias*, brought to him.

The chief ordered the assembled doctors and nurses to give injections of poison to all of the sick who were found in the hospital in order to make a quicker end of them. The doctors tried to save the situation with the pretext that they did not have the appropriate injections. The chief's answer to this was that if everything was not taken care of in the course of two hours, he would order the sick to be shot along with all of the hospital personnel.

After a long and painful consultation, the doctors decided to kill the sick by injection.

The chief doctor of the hospital, the surgeon Dabczinski, gave out the first order, that his mother should poison her mother, that is, his grandmother. His mother, who lived in the hospital building, had put poison in a glass of tea and given it to her mother to drink. When the old one began to writhe in agony, the doctor, her grandson, gave her an injection, from which she immediately fell asleep forever. Her daughter covered herself with tears and wished that her hand be punished if she had committed an error, poisoning her own mother.

p. 174

The sick were forced to be poisoned and permit the injections. Those who struggled were forcefully poisoned. The doctors and the nurses worked at hastening the deaths of the sick with tears in their eyes and when everyone lay dead, the doctors and all of the hospital personnel stood over those who had just been alive and now were dead people and mourned. They lamented their actions and themselves.

It was reported to the chief that no sick remained in the hospital, only the dead. He replied: "Yes, it is good!"

He chose a large number of the personnel and sent them to the train wagons. The doctors and the rest of the youngest and prettiest female personnel he sent to quarantine.

Then the chief made a visit to another hospital – of epidemic diseases. Dr. Kagan, the director of the hospital, had tried to have all of the sick standing up for the duration of the *aktsia*. But now, during the fifth *aktsia*, all of the sick and the greater number of hospital personnel were sent away to the train wagons. Only some of the personnel were taken to quarantine.

After finishing with the hospital, the chief went to find all of the Jews who had contact with the Germans. He found Kolenbrener, the well known, elegant young man, the director of the Jewish housing office, who had been hiding in a factory for a few days, and said that he should be taken to a train wagon. Then he asked that Wajnrib, the *Judenrat* member, who was well known among the Gestapo members and who had hidden him, be found. The chief's people did find him and brought him. The chief then ordered that all Jews who were named Wajnrib – women, men and children and Wajnrib's entire family, his wife and children, his brothers, sisters and their families – be immediately brought and everyone was sent away to the wagons.

p. 175

Furthermore, they also looked for all the other lesser well-known men and women who had some connection with the Gestapo and all were deported.

At the very end, the chief and his driver and close assistants left for the artisans' house, *Aleja* number 14. There they first created a great tumult in the courtyard and shrieked that all Jewish residents should quickly go down to the courtyard and leave their residences open. The artisans and their wives and children descended, each with their papers in their hand. The men were ordered to line up according to their individual workshops. Each master craftsman with his family and the people registered on the paper of the city chief stood apart. But the chief did not look at the papers. He asked each one how old he was and what his occupation was. He ordered the very young men and women to line up separately and the old ones and the children also separately. I and my wife and child and three women, who were registered on our paper, stood together. The chief asked me how old I am - I answered him, 40; a factory master craftsman by profession. Then he looked at my wife and child and said, "You must separate."

My wife was so surprised that she could not utter a word. I said for her: "My wife is a master craftswoman in the hat workshop." He said of this, "That does not matter to me now!" He went on to another family and my people were placed in a group of the old and children by the gendarmes. We saw that he was choosing very young people and the mass of artisans and their families would be sent to the train wagons.

p. 176

After inquiries and sorting out young and old, he said to everyone:

– You come away! The old people are going to a camp and you, the young, will work. Your work will not necessarily be tailoring and the making of sample clothing. Other work will be found for you.

Everyone's faces grew pale and no one could utter a word. It became deadly still. But in the same moment steps were heard. We saw Mrs. Maszewicz arrive. She remained standing for a while, until the chief went to her. They remained standing in the distance for several minutes and talked. Then the chief came back to us with slow steps and began to search the rows for old people. They were tense, tragic seconds. We saw that fate had fallen only on the old people.

After the selection of the old people in the rows, he again turned to everyone and said: go back to your residences, help the people to dress and they should be here in the courtyard with their things in 10 minutes. They are leaving.

He told all of the young, earlier chosen men and women to return with everyone to the residences. Everyone departed and only the gendarmes and their chief remained in the courtyard.

Heartbreaking scenes occurred in the residences of the old people on which the bitter fate had fallen. We saw through the windows that the chief was looking at his watch and then in the window. A gendarme immediately shouted: "*Herunter* [Down]!" And we saw the first two old people coming down to the courtyard - the master craftsman from the knitting workshop,

p. 177

Fajgenblat and his wife. They wiped their tears and made hand movements to the window of their residence, where stood their two sons and their wives and beautiful grandson, who screamed: "*Zeydeshi! Bobeshi!* [Grandfather, grandmother] Stay here with us! Do not go away!" The child cut through the atrocious stillness of the courtyard, where the chief and his servants were moving about, with his sharp voice.

Brandlewicz, the tailor, joined the old couple, with his wife and 10-year old grandson, whose parents had been deported during an earlier *aktsia*. They also looked up to the second story to their dear daughter and beautiful grandchildren. From another exit came the pious seamstress, dressed in her *sheitl* [wig worn by pious married women], and her husband, the son of the rabbi in Klobuck, with their packs on their shoulders. They walked and cried. They were still young people; what did the murderer want from them? He did not like their appearance.

The old Frank, who had come to his son here, moved closer to the unfortunate people. Also a sturdy, tall man of 51, the husband of Wolfowicz, the corset maker. The chief asked him what his occupation was. He answered: "My wife makes corsets." Everyone knew that he was a locksmith. What had happened was that he became afraid and did not know what to say. The chief did not like his answer and he was chosen to be sent away.

A little later, through the window we saw that opposite the third story, the furrier, Goldsztajn, and his wife, the tailor Gryn's father-in-law and mother-in-law descended to the courtyard with packs on their shoulders. It seems that it did not help that their son-in-law, Gryn, the tailor and policeman, had such a good acquaintance with Chief Degenhardt.

p. 178

The group of people in the courtyard kept growing larger. Lensinski, the tailor, arrived with his wife and the best journeyman tailor from the woman's tailoring workshop, Haimke - an older Jew with his pack on his work worn shoulders. Everyone lined up in a row. Their children still wanted to talk with them, but the gendarmes did not permit it. The children only were able to give them money and food, which they had forgotten to take with them.

Suddenly there was a tumult. Several gendarmes ran down to a cellar and screamed. In a short time they led up four women and a young boy of 12 from there. Those who had been caught were brought to the group that stood ready to leave. As it turned out, the women and the child had arrived in the house after the list of the additional people had been closed and it was no longer possible to add them. Because they were afraid of remaining during the *aktsia*, they had hidden in the cellar. At the last minute, someone must have denounced them and they were found. The gendarmes wanted to shoot them immediately in the cellar, but because the mother-in-law of an assistant to the Jewish police was also there and she had strongly pleaded that her life be spared, citing her son-in-law, the gendarmes agreed to also bring them up to the courtyard and send them away with the group.

The group consisted of 19 people. The gendarmes counted them off and ordered them to leave the house. Their sons, daughters, grandchildren, relatives, acquaintances and all of the artisans stood at the windows. Everyone took leave from afar with tears in their eyes.

On another day, Mrs. Maszewicz told the artisans that the *aktsia* passed in the artisans' house "for the best." She assured them that right in the courtyard, at the last minute she convinced the chief that he should not take more than 10 percent for deportation. As there were 190 registered people, he took 19. If she had not arrived, he would have taken 90 percent and he would have sent 10 percent of the young people to the metallurgy workshop as they wanted to liquidate the artisans' house. At the last minute she convinced him that the artisans' house should continue to be active.

The fenced in work camp HASAG.

p. 179

Chapter XXXIV

The New Ghetto

The ghetto remained empty after the fifth *aktsia*, a result of which 35,000 Jews were deported from our city. The houses were empty, the shops closed. From my second story high balcony in the artisans' house, I saw the guards going through the ghetto streets. They were guarding against looting by the Polish population of the belongings that were left behind by the deported Jews.

Chief Degenhardt ordered the creation of a "new ghetto," smaller than the previous one, that would take in the Jews who still remained after the *aktsias*. He assigned the former *Judenrat* president to create a new *Judenrat*, smaller than the earlier one, and he ordered the assistants from the police to create a police precinct from the remaining 50 Jewish policemen.

All of the slave laborers from the factories and all of those in quarantine – the doctors and their families and the nurses and the remaining personnel from the hospital – had to be brought to the new, smaller ghetto.

p. 180

The chief discovered three small streets, dirty, without plumbing and without sewers and ordered the newly organized Jewish representation to create a new ghetto here.

The Jewish workers buried tall posts of wood around the three ghetto streets under the supervision of the Jewish police, shoving in the blocks every three or four meters and enclosed them with barbed wire. A wider area was left over for a gate.

Thus, the new ghetto was created.

The *Judenrat* "organized" anew again. The agile influential people allotted themselves "offices" and they proceeded to their "activities."

The *Judenrat* allocated residences for six to eight people in a room or for three or four couples together. "Furniture" was also apportioned – old broken tables and chairs – because anything that was still good was removed by the Germans to their warehouses.

A kitchen was set up. The chief appropriated products for it from the managing committee and thus again was organized the new wretched life.

During the cleaning out of the residences on the three new ghetto streets, hiding places were found from which Jews emerged - men, women, young people and children. The people there had lived in the worst, most terrible conditions, but they were hidden. They were lucky because here they would be in the ghetto again and they would be among Jews. They would still need to hide from the chief and his gendarmes who still came here, but it was easier for them. Death no longer hovered before their eyes as before and they would receive food and they could wash themselves.

The dead were also taken out of the hiding places – those who had not endured the terrible conditions and also children, some who had died and others who were suffocated so that they would not betray [the hiding place] with their crying.

p. 181

Still more people began to emerge from the bunkers that were found on other streets in the earlier ghetto. The food reserves had been finished off. These people were shot on the spot. When the emergence from the holes took on a mass character, the chief ordered that the people be brought to a collection camp on Katedralne Street. This caused suspicions that the chief again was organizing an *aktsia*.

Several days later, the chief did order the deportation to Radomsko of 800 Jewish souls who had been gathered in the collection camp. They were to be sent farther from there with the local Jews.

After the emptying of the collection camp, the chief gave an order that all Jews who were found in the bunkers be shot on the spot. After the order, each day brought fresh victims.

p. 181

Chapter XXXV

From Ghetto to Labor Camp

The new, smaller ghetto did not exist for long; the designation of "ghetto" was abolished and it was given the name "*Judenarbeitslager*" [Jewish labor camp].

The white bands with the *Mogen Dovid* [Shield of David, usually referred to as the Star of David] on the right arm were abolished in the labor camp and also in the artisans' house on *Aleja* number 14. However, simultaneously, the names of the Jews were "abolished." Everyone became nameless and every Jew received a tin number, which he had to wear on his chest. The Jews felt still more degraded and dejected.

p. 182

At the beginning of the month of December 1942, Chief Degenhardt ordered all of the Jewish doctors to appear at the large square of the former ghetto. The doctors became anxious because of the order, but all appeared at the spot indicated. The chief explained that there were many Jews in Radomsko and there was a lack of doctors there. Therefore, the German regime located there requested six doctors from the Czenstochow "labor camp." And since there were too many here, he would send them there. It should be understood that he did not ask anyone who wanted to go, but he himself chose six doctors and notified them that they and their wives and children should be ready to leave for Radomsko in a few days. The chief was very polite during the conversation and smiled considerably. He said that the six doctors who would go there would be grateful to him in three weeks because it would be so good for them there. Naturally, no one asked why they would be thankful to him in three weeks.

Several days later the chief exchanged two of the earlier chosen doctors for another two. It was said that it smelled of someone's hand from the *Judenrat* because everyone believed that it was better to remain here in the "labor camp" than to go somewhere to an unknown fate.

The doctors were sent away in the middle of December. They lined up with their wives and children on the square where trucks were waiting for them.

The *Judenrat* came out to take leave of them and to give them food and warm clothing. The remaining doctors and other Jews stood in the "labor camp" – this former ghetto – right at the wires, from where they said goodbye to the departing doctors with tears in their eyes.

Everyone had a bad premonition; at the last minute, the chief came to the square and again said that in three weeks the doctors would be grateful to him.

The residents of the artisans' house were not supposed to leave the house. However, they could declare to the Jewish assistants from the police who lived in the same house that they needed to go to the doctor. Then they were taken to the "labor camp" and back by a Jewish policeman. In addition, the artisans from the house could spend time with those closest to them and their acquaintances in the "labor camp." After the first visit to the "labor camp," each of the artisans returned from there broken. I also wanted to see the "labor camp" and, therefore, on a certain afternoon I went with the others.

p. 183

Chapter XXXVI

In the "Labor Camp"

We went in twos, led by a Jewish policeman, one pair behind the other; altogether 10 people.

We went in the middle of the road on the bridge like horses and plodded in the mud. The passing Poles looked in our eyes, acquaintances no longer greeted us, but smiled from the distance. Non-acquaintances laughed in our faces and shouted curse words after us. Grown young Poles ran after us and shouted not only at us, but also at the policeman such insulting words that would insult the honor of each of us.

We went along the amply long Wilson Street in this manner until the end. Here we entered the first street of the former ghetto. The street was named "Krutka." There we saw a terrible picture:

p. 184

The windows of the houses in which Jews had been found not too long ago stood open. The windowpanes were broken. The frames dangled on the half pried loose iron bars. The wind blew in and out of the rain-soaked drapes and roller blinds. The sound of doors banging back and forth inside was heard. The wind ran from house to house, from apartment to apartment and from room to room. The gates of the houses were thrown wide open and as we went by, we looked deeper into the courtyard. We could see broken pieces of furniture, photographs and portraits. Various *seforim* [religious books] – *khumishim, gemaras, siddurim, maksorim** were scattered on the street in front of the gates. In the gutters – pots, bowls and other crockery. The doors of several shops were ripped open and remnants of the goods lay around. It was evident that the shops had been plundered and only the least important things were left.

*[*The Five Books of Moses*, rabbinical commentaries, prayer books and prayer books for Rosh Hashanah and Yom Kippur.]

So were we, the 10 people, led by the Jewish policeman, passing streets where thousands of Jews had once lived, where Jewish life sparkled, where almost every open window was a reminder of a friend and an acquaintance. But now everything was empty and deserted. We did not see a living soul. We passed the square that was called the "small Warsaw market." Again we saw empty, deserted houses. From this market we came to the "labor camp" and stopped at the large gate. A quartermaster, a tall, stocky person with a red face, appeared and asked: "*Wer sind die bummel-manner?*" That is, who are the idlers? The Jewish policeman answered him that he had brought 10 people from the artisans' house to the doctor. We found out that the person was the chief of the "labor camp" and he was named Uberschaer. The Jewish policemen thought highly of him. They said that he would drink and eat with several of them, but that did not stop him from shooting Jews at every opportunity and beating them for the least trifle.

p. 185

We entered through the large gate, before which stood a Polish policeman on the side of the market and a Jewish policeman inside the camp.

I went into one of the three small and filthy streets. I met several Jewish policemen who looked at me with suspicion, as if they would say: "What are you doing here?" Then I met a policeman I knew, who told me I should be careful because from daybreak until 5 in the evening, no one was permitted to be found in the street. Everyone had to be at work. Only the Jews who work in the factories at night could move through the streets of the "labor camp." They wore special yellow bands on their arms with the inscription "night shift." If a Jew was found in the street during the work hours, he would be shot.

The policeman told me that the chief, Degenhardt himself, came here very often. He strolled around and searched. He asked that the houses be opened and checked for anyone who might be hiding. Once he found two young people in a residence. One was from the "night shift" and the other – a weak person, who could not go to work on that particular day. The chief ordered that the young man from the "night shift" be taken to the German guard and that the second one be shot.

It was three o'clock in the afternoon. Therefore, I waited in the room of my policeman acquaintance until it would be five. His residence was found in a house that was specially assigned to Jewish policemen. They lived there with their families, each family in a separate room. The more distinguished lived in two rooms. The wives of the policemen were freed from work; they were also permitted to "legally" have small children with them (this was a "privilege"), but all were full of worry about their future fate. Each mother sought advice about how to send their child over to the "Aryan side." They had a premonition that the chief in the "labor camp" would not leave any children. He could not see any soul who did not work. They also did not believe that he would let those working live. In general, they were skeptical about the fate of the entire "labor camp."

p. 186

Suddenly I heard a faint noise behind the door. The woman came out of the room and immediately came back with her husband to whom she said: "The father can remain here; the Jew is an acquaintance of ours from the artisans' house."

Hearing the woman call the person entering *"Tata,"* [father], I looked at him to see if I knew the woman's father. But it was difficult for me to recognize him because the Jew had changed so much. Before the war he was the vice-president of the Jewish *kehile* [organized Jewish community] in Czenstochow, a Jew in his 70's, with a long, wide beard. He had had a fancy goods business in the best neighborhood in the city. Now, I saw him clean-shaven; his grey hair was colored black; his wide figure seemed as if shrunken. He told me with tears in his eyes that he was there with his wife. They lay hidden in a cellar for entire days and nights and could no longer bear the hardship. I also wanted to see his wife and, therefore, waited until it got dark. His daughter went for her and brought her into the room. She entered quietly – She explained to me, "We have to watch out for our own Jews." The woman recognized me immediately. However, I had to look carefully until I recognized her as the once beautiful and kindhearted woman. She told me that for her all of life had been made unpleasant; she persevered only because that is how her daughter wanted it, but she could no longer bear so much pain.

p. 187

The two older people burst into tears like small children. They were sorry that they had not gone along with all of the other Jews to Treblinka. Their son-in-law, the policeman, had tried with all of his strength and means to hide them in holes, in attics; he led them from one place to another, from one gate to another, bribed gendarmes, in order to save them, until they finally were brought here to the "new ghetto," the present "labor camp." They could not be given a residence because they were "illegal" and did not have numbers. They had to hide, but they lived in constant fear because they knew that in the end the murderers would come here and discover their victims.

It was already very dark when I went outside. The alleys of the "labor camp" were poorly lit. I encountered an acquaintance who was a conductor of the *TOZ* [Society for the Protection of Health] choir. We were both delighted that we were both still alive. He invited me to his residence. We went through the alleys and I heard Jews call out: "Meat to sell! Fresh bread, fresh rolls and bagels, wurst, herring, sugar, whiskey!"

I went closer and saw the workers who had just then returned from work. Now they had become traders. They brought all of the things from the "Aryan side." There they bought or exchanged things for clothing items and here they sold them again. The prices were high. Wurst was produced in the "labor camp." We went through a large courtyard, over hills and holes, through back entrances and back doors. A Jew stood every few steps and told the customers what was available today. They took great care about who was coming, against whom they must protect themselves. Today there were small sausages. Customers went in and out. Everything happened very quietly and carefully; for producing wurst, one received the death penalty. But the earnings were such that they risked their lives, because life was constantly at risk anyway.

p. 188

In other streets, Jews were selling pants, coats, underwear and every sort of clothing. This was merchandise that was gathered every day from the abandoned Jewish houses and taken to the large warehouses on Garibaldi Street. The Jewish things from the former ghetto were sorted by Jews who worked like slaves. In order to stay alive, these slave workers – good, well-raised Jewish children – risked their lives and "stole" things, putting them on at their departure from work. They risked their lives in this way every day, because they were stealing Jewish clothing from the Germans.

I went up with my friend to his residence, which consisted of a room and a kitchen. Seven wooden and iron beds appeared before me, some propped up with pieces of wood. Four women were hanging around. It was very crowded. There were few chairs on which to sit. They mainly sat on the beds.

I saw a young man lying in one bed. I asked my friend why the Jew was lying in bed, if he was sick.

The sick one answered me himself: "There is nothing wrong with me. I lie in bed out of boredom."

He wondered why I did not recognize him. I started to look closer at him and saw a man with a thinned out face, with a skullcap on his head, but I could not recognize him.

Then the man said to me:

"I am the local city *khazan* [cantor] - former."

I shuddered. Is this the *khazan*? The *khazan* with the wide beard, with the long, wide face; the *khazan* who would proudly go through the Jewish neighborhood every Friday night and *Shabbos* on his way to the synagogue for prayer?

p. 189

How different he had become. Nothing like the same person.

I did not ask him anything about his family. I was afraid to touch a painful spot. However, unasked, he himself began to tell me:

- I have become a young man - he said with bitterness.

His wife and his seven children, each smaller than the next, were deported. Now he must look young; he is recorded as a 25-year old. The beard is shaved off. He has become much thinner. Some sort of new person has grown, nothing like the earlier one. A Jew who had a wife and seven children has become a young man!

Suddenly he sat up quickly in bed. His face became red as if blood has poured in. He balled up his fists and screamed wildly:

- The murderers! They have made me young! Made me a young man! Annihilated my seven children! Murdered my wife!

His fury tore him out of bed. He quickly got dressed, thus tearing his suit jacket. Then he sat down at the table and immediately stood up again – he could not find a place for himself.

My friend winked at me. I should start talking to him about something else in order for him to calm himself. I tried to do this, but he did not let me. He could not forget his grief. He began to pace around the room, speaking as if to himself:

– Everyday I go to work; I am a slave. I work in a factory. What good is all of this? Why am I still living? To be a slave for the Germans!

Some of the other residents of the house sat at the corner of the table and put down bread. At another corner two couples who lived there ate. Everyone ate by themselves. The benches were surrendered to those who wanted to sit and eat. Four couples and four "young men" lived in the apartment. During the day they all were at work, both men and women. At night they came together and brought soup with a piece of bread from the kitchen and whoever had money bought other things in the street.

p. 190

My acquaintance, the orchestra conductor, a very dear person, told me that his wife and child were deported and he was alone. Life was very tiresome for him; what should he do, he had no courage to end his life, but he would willingly do it.

I realized that I had to be at the exit of the "labor camp" at seven o'clock in order to go home with my group. However, it was now seven thirty. I took leave of my friend and quickly went down to the wire fence where I learned that my group had gone home half an hour ago. I had no other choice but to spend the night in the "labor camp" and leave there in the morning with a group of workers that would leave for work. In the "labor camp" it was permissible to be in the street until nine o'clock. I slowly went through the alleys and met still more acquaintances who I told of my situation. One of them took me along and said that he would provide me with a place to sleep on the floor in a corner. He said that one could sleep like that for one night. A Jew can do everything!

I entered a large room in which six people lived, three men and three women. Young women who remained without husbands and men who remained without their wives. They had decided to live together and to get married. It was difficult for both the men and the women to live alone. Each of them had experienced great misfortune, but the will to live was great and they were looking to survive.

p. 191

Here I saw a young, beautiful woman who was in her own villa before the war with her husband and two beautiful children. Now she lived in the room for six people – along with a young man the same age as she. Each of them was at work the entire day; at night the woman cooked food; they occupied a third of the room. Their furniture consisted of a bed and a little cabinet with its back of plain boards facing the room. This was supposed to hint at a kind of curtain that divided their small piece of living space from the rest of the room.

My acquaintance "lived" in a second corner of the room with a young woman who became an orphan during an *aktsia*. He had had a wife and two children. Having earlier been a policeman, he showed his family how to hide. But during the *aktsia* when he was on "duty," a gendarme uncovered his family and took them away to the railroad car. Now he had married the young orphaned woman.

The third corner of the room was occupied by a young man with his wife. The young man had always been a worker without any specialty. His wife and child were deported during the third *aktsia*; he married his wife's sister who remained all alone. This young man earned more than the others living with him. He became a foreman and removed the things from the former ghetto to the warehouses on Garibaldi Street. Every day he had the opportunity to hide various things that he brought home and gave to those living with him to sell when they went to their workplaces. They brought home money from the things or bartered them for food products. The three couples ate well, drank alcohol and smoked. They wanted to forget everything that was and not think of what would happen.

p. 192

An oven for cooking stood in the fourth corner of the room that was used by everyone. In the middle of the room stood a large table with benches around it that were used by everyone.

They told me that rumors were going around that a further *aktsia* soon would be carried out. The chief had someone say that he knew of several people and children who were hidden in the "labor camp." But nothing was known for certain.

That evening I sat at a large table in a large room together with a little too many people for such a room and conversed in an almost cozy manner. A roasted goose was on the table and a liter of whiskey. The window shudders were closed; the doors were locked and sometimes for the moment it seemed that people were sitting here as in normal times and were spending time – in a somewhat primitive manner, but normal and cozy.

The people wanted to convince themselves and each other that they had forgotten what had happened to them and around them during the last few weeks and they did not want to think about what would happen – "They only wanted to live and nothing more!"

But it was really very different. A heavy stone pressed deep in their hearts and it did not stop torturing them for one second.

When the first glass of whiskey was emptied, one after the other, the women took out their handkerchiefs and began to wipe their eyes, unnoticed at first, then the tears began to fall rapidly and finally they wept loudly.

p. 193

– Why are you crying? – the "new" husband asked his "new" wife who had lost her two children at the *aktsia*.

The wife stood up from the table, shook and fell onto the bed with a heartrending cry.

– Where are my children now? – She cried almost hysterically.

My friend's eyes filled with tears at the word "children." He turned toward a corner of the room and stealthily started to wipe his eyes. Little by little he came closer to the door and left the room in order to cry for his wife and two little daughters. As a man, he probably thought it not "suitable" to cry in front of everyone like a woman.

Finally, the woman who had married her sister's husband also cried and the entire room was filled with sorrow and crying.

The Nazi murderer, Heinrich Kestner, who liquidated the small ghetto in a bloody way
(Photographed after his arrest, when Czenstochow was liberated by the Polish military)

The roasted goose remained uneaten; the whiskey was not drunk and everyone went to sleep.

I lay down on the floor in a corner near the oven. In the late night quiet I heard deep sighs. When one woman sighed deeply, another immediately sighed as if answering, then the third one. Finally the men accompanied them and sighing was heard from all of the corners. That is how the life of the new married couples appeared.

I could not fall asleep and listened to the low ticking of the clock. When it struck five, I heard a trumpet similar to that which I would hear when serving in the military – in the morning to be awakened and at night at going to sleep.

Everyone woke up quickly and got up from bed. My acquaintance took a large pot and went out to the street. He came right back with black coffee. Everyone got dressed quickly, drank a little coffee and placed over their arms the wide sacks with wide stripes of sackcloth. No one had any more time to speak to me. Each one rushed to their work group.

p. 194

I went to the exit of the "labor camp." There was great movement there; there were masses of people on the square and each one looked for his group. All were lined up in rows of three; each group had a leader. The director of the work places stood at the gate with a note and counted how many people there were in each group. The chief of the "labor camp," the sergeant major, stood on the other side of the gate. All of the passing Jews greeted him, taking off their hats from their heads. He stopped several groups: something did not please him. Someone's sack was too thick. He searched several, giving someone a slap in his face and screamed with screeching shouts.

Thus several thousand slaves left the "labor camp" for various workplaces.

I left with a group of workers who were going to the artisans' house.

*　　*

*

Chief Degenhardt ordered the *Judenrat* to put together a list of the Jews who had relatives in *Eretz-Yisroel*. It was said that this had a connection with an exchange between Germany and England; the exchange would be of Germans who were in England for Jews from the General Government.

Others again suspected that the chief would fool people with the list and they would be sent who knew where. It was again unclear why he needed to "fool" us with lists when he could do whatever he wanted to do with us.

p. 195

The registration began. The *Judenrat* put together several lists. A separate list of children who had parents there; of those who had brothers or sisters, fathers or mothers; then a separate list of those who had distant relatives there.

Many people registered for these lists.

Several days after the registration we learned that there was an unease in the "labor camp." One day, the Jewish policemen who lived with us in the artisans' house came for lunch. They said that after the work groups who work outside the "labor camp" went to their workplaces, the chief came and ordered that every Jew who remained at his workplace in the "labor camp," namely, in the *Judenrat*, in the kitchen, in the hospital, in the warehouses and in the laundry – should line up at the small market.

When they were all assembled, the chief chose 200 young men and sent them with the Polish policemen to the German sentries.

The policemen were not able to tell us what had happened to the people; they only knew that people who had committed some sort of sin were usually sent there and no one had come back from there. And as the 200 young people had not sinned in any way, this was something new and therefore a despondent mood reigned.

The people were under arrest for three days. None of their close relatives were permitted to see them. They received food from the kitchen through the Polish policemen; they slept on the bare ground.

p. 196

Several trucks from an ammunition factory in Skarzysko* arrived at the small market and the young people were loaded into them. Two young men tried to escape during the loading and they were shot.

*[Translator's note: Skarzysko-Kamienna was the site of an ammunition factory built in 1924. During the Second World War, the factory became part of the German HASAG concern – Hugo Schneider *Metallwarenfabrik AG* of Leipzig – and was used as a forced labor camp. Many Jewish prisoners were poisoned by their work with the highly toxic picric acid that was used for munitions and explosives.]

In a week, on a Sunday, a Pole from Skarzysko came to my room and gave me 20 letters and a special letter to me from my cousin who was sent away with the young people and was told to give all of the letters to the wives and families of those sent away.

We learned from the letters that the young people were sent to work in the ammunition factory in Skarzysko. Immediately after their arrival, their clothing and everything they had with them was taken from them and they were given paper suits. There they had to work with chemical materials that harmed the lungs and under very difficult conditions. The food was very bad and scarce and they had to sleep on the bare ground. Whoever became ill was shot.

All of the letter writers asked those closest to them to send money with the bearer of the letters, a Polish worker in that factory, who was free on Sunday and, therefore, he could bring the letters.

I gave the letters to the relatives of the deported with the help of a Jewish policeman. The terrible news about the labor camp in Skarzysko spread immediately. The wives and closest relatives of the young men in Skarzysko sent two women who brought letters and money for their close ones to the artisans' house. The Polish worker took everything. He received 20,000 *zlotys* for the men and 2,000 for his trouble and he returned to Skarzysko on the same night.

Chapter XXXVII

Again an *Aktsia*

The Death of Two Heroes

On the 4th of January 1943 we heard from the work group that came from the "labor camp" to the artisans' house just as every other day that every group was thoroughly checked that day at the exit gate. People, who had to take care of something on the "Aryan side," would always enter our house with the people in the work group. The people would sit with an artisan and wait for their Polish acquaintances who came here. (The artisans' house was the only Jewish house in which "Aryans" were permitted to enter.) All of the artisans' rooms and also the corridors were always occupied with waiting people. The artisans willingly helped with what they could.

This time, however, none of these people came because they were not permitted through the gates of the "labor camp."

At around noon, through the windows of the artisans' house we saw coal wagons and garbage wagons packed with Jewish children. They were traveling in the direction of the Polish police commissariat on Pilsudski Street. Then we immediately saw large groups of Jews half dressed, without coats, led by gendarmes with pointed rifles with bayonets. The Jews went with their hands raised in the air.

The artisans became uneasy. The children were afraid. No one knew what would happen. We waited for the Jewish policemen who would come here every day at noon, but they did not come on this day and that increased our unease.

p. 198

It was clear that some sort of *aktsia* was taking place in the "labor camp."

The policemen came home at night and we learned what had happened that day:

Immediately in the morning, Rohn, the lieutenant of the gendarmerie, the chief's representative, came to the "labor camp" and ordered that a thorough check be made at the exit so that not one Jew would be permitted to leave the camp with the workers. After the workers marched out, the "labor camp" became quiet until 10 o'clock. Then the lieutenant ordered that all of those remaining in the "labor camp" should go to the small market. The Jewish police again received the order to gather all of the children and to bring them there. When the police did not carry out the order quickly enough, the lieutenant called them together and declared that each one of them would be responsible with his life if he did not produce at least two children. The policemen went to the "labor camp" with heavy hearts to search for children.

The gendarmes searched through all of the houses to see if anyone was hidden. Those found were murderously beaten and dragged to the small market.

At the market, Lieutenant Rohn surrounded the Jews with gendarmes and began to choose men and women who were placed on one side. He ordered the gendarmes to take whatever they found in their pockets or hidden in their clothing.

The lieutenant again chose among the people until he came upon a young man of 18 named Fajner.

p. 199

The young man had lost his parents during an *aktsia*. The lieutenant ordered Fajner to leave the row and stand with those who had been chosen. The young man left and shouted to all the assembled Jews:

– We have had enough suffering from the murderers! We will no longer let them slaughter us!

At that moment he pulled out a revolver from his pocket and aimed it at the lieutenant. But the revolver jammed and did not fire.

Immediately, one of the other young men of his age stepped out, and seeing that the revolver did not fire, ran to the lieutenant and began to cover him with blows and slaps.

This did not last long. The gendarmes drew back a little and pointed their rifles toward the assembled. One pulled the revolver out of Fajner's hands with his foot and shot a bullet into him. With the bullet in his body, Fajner again ran and helped his friend in his struggle with the lieutenant. However, he immediately lost his strength and he fell down on the ground. Then, he moved toward the lieutenant on his stomach, grabbed him by the coat and pulled him toward himself, screaming: "You murderer!" At that moment gendarmes shot eight bullets into Fajner and he breathed out his soul.

Those assembled, around 300 people, stood as if frozen. In an instant there was a shout to them: "Hende hoch!" [Hands high] And everyone raised their hands. The gendarmes ran toward them and searched for weapons, but none of them had any more weapons.

Meanwhile, the second man was also shot and fell on the snow next to his friend.

The lieutenant had got on his bicycle and left. He returned in a few minutes with a larger squad of gendarmes.

p. 200

Meanwhile, the Jewish policemen searched all of the hiding places. They knocked out doors and windows of the homes where they noticed children hidden by parents who were at work. The frightened children hid deeper under the beds, in attics and stalls. They crawled into holes, but each policeman had to bring two children and he had to find them. Each policeman dragged through the streets two children, who cried and begged: "Wait until my *mameshi* [mommy] comes. She will pay for me."

The childish talk cut the hearts, but was of no help and 150 children stood in the "small market" in a great frost, half undressed, without coats, with frozen fingers. They cried and screamed: "*Mameshi!*" It could move a stone, but not Lieutenant Rohn. He ordered his assistants to throw the children in the garbage wagons and to take them to the Polish commissariat.

Later, the half wild Rohn approached the people who were standing with their hands in the air and choose 25 of the handsomest and best physically developed men from there. They were placed in rows of four and forced to a wall near the wire fencing. Gendarmes with rifles stood there and shot them. At the last minute, each of the young men shouted to the bandits: "Criminals!" Murderers!" "You will yet lose the war!" and similar outcries.

When the 25 young men lay on the ground, two gendarmes with revolvers in their hands went among the dead and shot them again. Then the other people with their hands in the air were taken to the Polish commissariat.

p. 201

At the time when the gendarmes looted the houses, two women, a mother and daughter, left their residence with the intention of going over to the "Aryan side." They took money and valuable things. However they were noticed by a gendarme. He shot after them and missed. The women remained standing and the thief ordered them to give him everything that they had. After taking everything from them, he told them to go farther, but just as they took the first step, he shot each of them twice and they fell to the earth dead.

Meanwhile, several thousand men and women returned from their workplaces. The men did not meet their wives and wives their husbands, the mothers – their children. If the men were not among those shot, they were in the police commissariat on the "Aryan side," where they would be shot or deported.

Heartrending scenes played out in the three alleys of the "labor camp." Women who had not found their husbands at home came to the place of the executions and searched among the dead; several women recognized their husbands and lost their minds. The entire "labor camp" behind the wire fencing was filled with crying and screaming.

In the evening, the 29 who tragically perished were buried.

By the light of candles in the dark and very frosty evening, the 27 martyrs were placed in a large grave and the mother and daughter nearby in a second grave.

The burial took a long time and those closest to those who perished and other people stood for a long time at the fresh graves and could not tear themselves away, until they were forced to leave.

p. 202

At the time when the burial of the annihilated took place in the "labor camp," the men, women and children, who had been brought to the Polish police commissariat, were tortured there. The Polish policemen took the victims into an office one by one and ordered them to undress completely, men as well as women. Everything that was found was taken from each one and then they were murderously beaten.

Early in the morning, Lieutenant Rohn entered the "labor camp" and ordered more children to be brought.

The chairman of the *Judenrat* turned to the lieutenant with a request to free several of the Jews who were at the Polish police commissariat, giving as a reason the fact that those people were needed for the work carried out by the *Judenrat.*

The lieutenant agreed on the condition that other Jews were put in their place. Therefore, the Jewish policemen captured other "less important" Jews and a few children and brought them to the commissariat.

The people who were going to be taken back to the "labor camp" as "necessary" stood in the courtyard of the police commissariat waiting for the other "unimportant" Jews and children who were supposed to ransom them. Among those who were supposed to be freed was a woman who a day earlier during the departure to the small market had hidden her two young sons, one seven and the other nine years old. When the people were brought who were supposed to ransom the "needed," her two children were among them. Seeing her standing in the courtyard, they got out of the wagon in which they were being taken, and began to shout: "Mama! *Mameshi!*"

p. 203

They became desperate; she was free – her children were doomed. The mother ran to her children and they to the mother and all remained together to be sent away.

It occurred in several cases that a Jew for whom liberation had been obtained was standing and waiting in the courtyard and he saw his wife among the newly arrived people. She had presented herself voluntarily to come here where her husband was found, not knowing that he would be freed. Here they were not allowed to go to each other. The man returned to the "labor camp" and the wife remained in the commissariat.

When the "exchange" was completed, the several hundred men, women and 200 children were sent to Radomsko, where the Jewish doctors had been sent several weeks earlier.

Several days later, four young men and two women in very sad condition entered the artisans' house. These people were escapees from the Radomsko ghetto. One young man was from Radomsko and the others from Czenstochow, who had been sent to Radomsko a few days before.

We learned the following from the young man from Radomsko: a while ago the General Governor in Krakow published an order that ghettos would be created in three cities, where Jews would be able to live because in many cities the ghettos had already been liquidated and Jews were not permitted to be found there. One of the three cities was Radomsko.

Because many Jews were found in the vicinity of Radomsko, hidden with peasants in the villages and living in constant fear of being denounced – they, hearing about the governor's announcement, began to move to Radomsko, so that in the course of two weeks, 5,000 Jewish souls arrived in the Radomsko ghetto.

p. 204

A *Judenrat* was created; residences were allocated and the Jews settled down. Little by little artisans began to work. The Polish population was permitted to enter the ghetto and food products were thus brought in. This lasted for two months.

However, suddenly the ghetto was closed. The Polish population was no longer permitted to enter and no Jew could go out.

It appeared that the General Governor's arrangements to fix up the ghetto was nothing more than a net to fool the Jews to come out of their hiding places. It was clear that everyone was waiting to be deported to Treblinka.

Some even began to make bunkers, but it was clear that they could no longer extract themselves from the net.

After the closing of the ghetto, Ukrainians arrived, taking over the supervision of the ghetto.

One morning, the *aktsia* took place. All of the Jews, over 5,000 souls, were chased from their residences and forced onto a large square in a burning frost. The several hundred Jews, adults and children from Czenstochow arrived for this *aktsia*. They stood under the open sky for long hours together with the Jews from Radomsko because the railway train with 16 cars that was to take them away was late. Meanwhile, the Gestapo and the Ukrainians ran around among the unlucky ones and robbed whatever they still possessed. It was in the afternoon that they were chased into the railway cars.

When the train was at full speed, several young people proceeded to cut out the wires from the little windows. However, in the wagon there reigned a mood of indifference and resignation. They tried to turn the young people away from their undertaking. But the young people made a great effort and tenaciously filed for hours until the wires of the little windows were sawn through and the six people sprang from the train into the darkness of the night. Some of them fell on soft snow; still others on wood and they severely bruised themselves. They decided not to travel together, but came back here to Czenstochow one by one and they arranged to meet in the artisans' house.

p. 205

Thus did the six young men (eight had jumped out, but two were still missing) arrive in Czenstochow through many efforts and another series of encounters on the way. They were sick and broken, their bodies wounded and their feet swollen. They remained in the artisans' house for three days and then went to the "labor camp" where they received medical help. On the first day they had to live there in secret until they were assigned to certain workplaces and again became slaves.

Several days later a young woman with a bound head arrived at the artisans' house at night. At first, we did not recognize her, but after a closer look, we saw that this was Mrs. Braun, the same one who had run to her two sons at the courtyard of the Polish police commissariat and, although, she could have been free, she had not wanted to leave her children, but went with them to Radomsko and from there in the railroad cars to Treblinka with all of the Jews.

She explained:

Several young men were in the railroad car, in which she traveled with her children, who after long hours of work had pulled out the wire-covered little windows and jumped out. Everyone in the wagon knew that they were going to Treblinka to their deaths. Therefore, everyone believed that whoever had the courage should save themselves by jumping out. She also wanted to save herself, but how could she jump with two children? Again she did not want to leave her children. But people in the wagon began to explain to her that everyone would perish in Treblinka, including the children. Therefore, it was better that at least she save herself. The two children sensed something and cuddled up to their mother. She kissed and calmed them until they fell asleep from exhaustion.

p. 206

Feeling freed from the children, the mother again went to the window that drew her as a magnet to steel. She looked out into the darkness and became frightened. The train was going fast and no one knew where they were. She again ran back to her children; she kissed them in their sleep and again went to the window. Several people, who saw her uncertainty, convinced her that in any case she would not be able to help her children in Treblinka and they pushed her to the window. She became dizzy and she suddenly jumped into the white snow.

She did not know for how long she lay unconscious. When she came to, she saw that she was lying in the middle of the night in an empty place. She sat up and felt a dampness on her forehead. She wiped it and saw blood by the light of the white snow. She placed snow on the wound on her head and wanted to stand up, but she immediately felt severe pain in her legs. There were also wounds on her legs. She also put snow on her legs and after lying for a while she slowly got up and began to put one foot in front of the other. She saw small candle flames in the distance and she slowly went in that direction. After a longer time she reached there and realized that she was at the Rogow train station near Warsaw. When she entered the train terminal she met a Polish train official. He recognized that she was Jewish and he hid her in his residence where she could wash and bandage her wounds. He bought a train ticket for her and placed her in the train for Czenstochow. She wanted to pay him with a piece of her clothing, but he did not want to take anything. That is how she came to Czenstochow.

p. 207

She rested a little with us in the artisans' house, but she did not stop crying. She felt guilty about her children.

In the morning she left for the "labor camp." There it was learned right away that she had jumped from the railroad car and left her children. Many condemned her for these deaths; others were sympathetic to her.

Two weeks later I met her in the "labor camp." She cried terribly and told me that she could not find any rest. Her two beautiful children with their hands held out to her were always before her eyes and they called to her constantly: "Mama, *mameshi!*"

The woman was despondent; she did not know what to do with herself. She had no one. Her husband had been murdered a long time ago by the Germans.

We went like this through the three "labor camp" alleys. Suddenly she remained standing in front of a passing Jewish policeman. She stopped him and asked:

– Is your name Szladowski?

– Yes. – The policeman answered.

– You pulled my children from under the bed in the locked residence and took them to the market to the *aktsia?*"

– Yes – the policeman answered – and you are the mother of the two beautiful young boys who left them in the railroad car in order to save yourself? As a policeman I was forced with the threat of death, which still torments me, but how could you, a mother, leave children and save yourself?

p. 208

Chapter XXXVIII

"Aryans" and "Muslims"

The Jews who still remained after all of the past *aktsias* took into account the constant danger that hung over them. They realized that they would not escape the evil fate and that the Germans would let them live only for as long as they could make them of use. Therefore, the thought arose among many that only those who could make themselves into "Aryans" would survive. In addition, however, one had to have an "Aryan" appearance and "Aryan papers."

In order to appear as an "Aryan," women with black hair dyed their hair blonde and men allowed thick whiskers to grow and they also dyed them blonde along with their hair.

As for "Aryan papers," they could be gotten through the recommendation of acquaintances, from particularly influential people who took large sums for this.

Poles would come to the artisans' house who took photographs and money from the Jews and after several days they brought ready made "Aryan papers" with birth certificates that showed that the person in question was an "Aryan" for endless generations.

But for the "Aryan appearance" and "Aryan papers," they still had to possess a great deal of money in order to remain in a strange city because they were afraid that in their own city, acquaintances and strangers would recognize the person and give him away.

p. 209

The majority of the Jews with "Aryan papers" went to the larger cities or to spas where it was easier to settle down. However, multitudes of blackmailers arose – Poles who specialized in finding "Aryan Jews." Such people would boldly and cockily approach someone in the street and say to him: "You are a Jew!" If the face of the Jew changed and he was startled, the blackmailer saw that he had guessed correctly and he demanded 10,000 *zlotes* or even more. If the Jew was able to pay, the matter was taken care of – at least for the present with this blackmailer. If, however, the Jew did not have any money, the blackmailer gave him to the Gestapo or police and the Jew was doomed.

The "Aryan Jews" who were caught were forced through torture to reveal their place of residence and the Gestapo would often at such opportunities discover the tracks of other false "Aryans" and of the manufacturers of "Aryan papers." In many cases, the Poles who had rented residences to the "Aryan Jews" were also shot together with the Jews.

Polish policemen also blackmailed and extorted money from Jews. If a Jew tried to insist that he was an "Aryan" he was taken to the Gestapo where it was verified if he was circumcised. Women were questioned as to whether they knew Catholic prayers and knew various religious customs.

Often a real Catholic with a Semitic appearance would be stopped. But they only received a bit of molestation on the part of the gendarmes and were freed.

Even though "Aryan papers" were an inadequate remedy, almost every Jew wanted to have them. They wanted to fool themselves because during a close inspection they were immediately seen to be a forgery. However, the fixers carried on a good business and they also found new ones. Thus they "invented" the creation of papers as Muslims who were also circumcised. Such papers were more expensive than the usual "Aryan ones" because it was thought that they were more secure. However, in reality the "Muslim" papers did not have the least worth because the German or Polish police immediately realized that they were dealing with an illegitimate "Muslim."

p. 210

But, the desperation of the Jews was so great that they grabbed at everything as a thirsty person to a straw.

A pile of ash remaining from the Czenstochow Ghetto
(New picture inserted in place of a poor quality image)

The destroyed synagogue named for the Czenstochow Rabbi, Nukhem Asz

p. 210

Chapter XXXIX

Three Ghettos

The chief issued a new decree that the men should be separated from the women in the "labor camp." He said that the men should live in Nadrzeczna Alley, the women in Kozia Street and married men and women in Garncarska Alley.

In this way the "labor camp" was divided anew into three ghettos.

The *Judenrat* again received a new task: carrying out the changes in residence of several thousand people.

These changes had to be carried out in the course of one week and then only at night when the workers came back from their work.

It had just become chilly and the people who came back from work hungry and frozen were forced to pull their poor little bits of furniture in the frost through slippery, small alleys – the beds and little cabinets – from one wet, cold room to a still worse apartment somewhere on Third Street, in a corner of a room with five or six other people.

p. 211

However, during this entirely horrible situation several *Judenrat* members were found who also had in mind the arrangement of better residences for women with whom they had "adulterous love affairs."

It is worthwhile to mention the fact that *Judenrat* members as a result of the general characteristics of the ghetto and of the "Jewish leaders" there – even some older family men with grown children – used the generally sad conditions and their "power" in order to find lovers among the lonely, unfortunate women who had lost their husbands or their parents. This "love" was won for the price of obtaining easier work in the "labor camp" and a better place to live.

It was not only "Jewish leaders," but also the chief himself who had a Jewish lover in the ghetto. During an *aktsia* her family was deported and she left the chief.

The Germans would call her "the beautiful Helenka." The chief had fixed up a beautiful residence for her in the ghetto. Every morning she went to the chief in the residence where she managed the house and in the evening she came back to the ghetto. Only she had the privilege of going to the entire city. The gendarmes and the policemen knew her.

On the morning when the "beautiful Helenka" celebrated her birthday, the chief sent her flowers with his servant-gendarme. The gendarme grumbled and said: What had love done to the chief – sending flowers to a Jewish girl!

p. 212

Chapter XL

The End of the Artisans' House

In the afternoon on one of the last days of the month of February 1943, the Gestapo suddenly entered the artisans' house. They went up to Zigelman, the furrier. After amusing themselves there for half an hour they arrested the furrier and his wife and a sister-in-law who had lost her husband during an *aktsia* and since then had lived with the Zigelmans.

The furrier's residence was searched and his nine-year old son remained alone in the courtyard without his parents and without a home.

Several days later it was learned that the three people had been shot at the cemetery.

The Gestapo came to the residence on several nights and took things from there until everything had been stolen. No one knew why the Zigelmans had been murdered.

The event made a heavy impression on the artisans. And several days later, when we learned that a house-search was being prepared for all of the artisans, the panic grew still greater.

Chief Degenhardt knew about the mood of panic among the artisans and he ordered the tailors Gryn and Kac to come to him. He visited a house with them at the old market that belonged to the "Aryan side" and he told them that he had decided to move the artisans from the house at *Allee* number 4 to this house. He further assured them that the new artisans' house would be spared exactly as during the previous *aktsias* and the house would not be part of the "labor camp" so that German clients would be able to visit it.

p. 213

The chief and the two tailors immediately selected a residence with a workshop for each artisan.

When the tailors returned, they informed the artisans that the residences in the new house were not really as comfortable as the present ones, but the situation would not change in any other way.

With this news, the mood in the artisans' house became calmer and everyone devoted himself to his work as before.

*   *

*

At six o'clock in the morning heavy military steps were heard in the courtyard of the artisans' house. Several minutes later there was a knocking on the doors of all of the Jewish residents and two gendarmes entered each residence, ordering the owners of the workshops to get dressed and to go down to the courtyard.

The gendarmes did not leave the residences, but carried out searches.

When the master craftsmen left their residences in order to go down to the courtyard, they met gendarmes and Ukrainians with weapons in their hands on the steps, corridors and in front of the house.

Chief Degenhardt stood in the middle of the courtyard with the sergeant major and gendarmes. When all of the Jewish master craftsmen were standing before him, he turned to them with this speech:

– From today on, the 9th of March 1943, the golden times for you, Jewish artisans from the house at *Allee* number 4 have ended. All of you will immediately move to the "labor camp" where you will live together with all of the Jews. I give you 20 minutes to gather your private clothing and to come down to the courtyard with your families. Goods, raw material, half and entirely completed work should be left in the residences. The keys should remain in the locks of the doors and cabinets.

p. 214

The chief no longer recognized Gryn, the tailor, whom he had made a policeman, nor the other tailor, who had visited him with the tailor Gryn, nor all of the other artisans for whom he had ostensibly designated the new house at the old market. "All Jews are equal!"

He left the house immediately, giving his people the proper instructions about how to carry out the *aktsia*.

The gendarmes waited 20 minutes. They made sure that no one from the artisans' house would take with him any goods, only private things. The artisans and their family members loaded themselves with packs over their shoulders and valises in their hands and went down to the courtyard. Approximately 200 people with their little bits of things stood in the courtyard and then began to march through the streets to the "labor camp." We were driven, guarded on all sides by the gendarmes and the Ukrainians, through Garibaldi Street where the large warehouses with the stolen Jewish things were located.

The greater number of those forced out could not carry their packs for long because the gendarmes and the Ukrainians made them go faster and faster. Therefore those who became more and more tired kept throwing away the goods that became heavier in the street and the gendarmes picked them up and brought them into the warehouses.

We were forced from Garibaldi Street through Warszawer Street where we did not see any civilians. There they still were cleaning out the businesses of the deported Jews. Only Polish policemen stood guard and laughed in our faces at how we were being pushed and chased and carrying our loads.

p. 215

A young man, sick with tuberculosis, lived in the artisans' house. He did not carry a pack and could not keep up with the fast pace. He remained behind; his wife dragged the packs on her weak shoulders and from time to time looked around at her very sick husband. He had a yellow complexion and he constantly held a hand at his heart. The murderers stepped on his feet and drove over them with their bicycles. However, he could not go faster. He could not even utter one word. One of the gendarmes took out his revolver and wanted to shoot the young man. However, the wife stopped and started to beg for him, that he was sick and could not walk. The gendarme deliberated and relented.

From Warszawer Street we entered the small market and from there, the "labor camp." There we found the alleys completely empty, without people. We were forced into a large hall on the first floor of the liquidated Jewish workshops. Everyone took off their packs and, tired, lowered themselves to the ground.

The artisans looked at each other as if surprised and confused. It was hard to understand that it was not long ago that we had lost our established home. We first dedicated ourselves to understanding that all of the assurances from our German clients and from Mrs. Maszewicz were deceptions in order to blind our eyes, just as the visit by the chief and the two tailors to the ostensibly new artisans' house was calculated so that no one would anticipate what would happen and take something out of the residence in time.

Meanwhile, several hours passed and we sat in a guarded house, not knowing what more would happen to us.

Finally, the chief arrived accompanied by a person from the Gestapo and called out that Kac, the tailor, and Szidlowski, the shoemaker, should go down to the ground floor with their families and to take their things with them. Understandably, the order was immediately carried out.

p. 216

Kac's small daughter came back up after several minutes and explained that downstairs the things were being searched and everyone had to completely undress for a search.

Everyone in the hall immediately took out their things of value and looked for some way in which to be rid of them because Jews were not supposed to have any large sums of money or valuables.

Seeking an alternative to help ourselves, we noticed a small window in the hall that looked onto a small courtyard. The courtyard bordered a second courtyard where we saw Jewish policemen and night workers who were looking up at us. We made signs to them with our hands and communicated to them the conditions in which we found ourselves. Many wrapped their money and valuables in a handkerchief, wrote their names on a piece of paper and threw it out of the small window. The others picked up the packets and immediately left.

But not everyone decided to do this with their money and valuables.

Meanwhile, we noticed through a second small window that the Kac and Szidlowski families were placed with their faces to a wall and after a while they were led away under heavy guard by the Ukrainians and gendarmes.

Then everyone on the first floor was called for a search. One by one they were led into a room where the chief and five gendarmes were found. The chief ordered everyone to turn over everything they owned and we were searched by the gendarmes only after this was done to see if, God forbid, we had hidden something.

After the search, we were let out with our things onto the street and each of us had to persuade an acquaintance somewhere that we be permitted to lay down our things.

p. 217

In this manner, the chief received 200 new people in the "labor camp" without money and without a roof over their heads. However, he left with a valise of money and valuables; as was later learned, he had taken 100,000 *zlotys*, in addition to the various items of value.

When the sick young man was searched and money was found on him, he received an order from the chief that he report to a doctor in the hospital.

The young man was taken into the hospital as a very sick person.

On another day, the chief went to the hospital and saw the young man laying on a bed and nearby in a small bed, another very ill man. The chief ordered the doctor to poison both of them.

A day later, when the chief spoke by telephone with his representatives about various matters, he did not forget to ask if the two sick men were already dead. When he received an answer that they were still alive, he issued an order that the Jewish police should bring the two sick men to be put under guard.

When two Jewish policemen arrived at the hospital for the sick men, everyone realized that they were being taken to be put under guard.

It was very bizarre in the hospital and no one wanted to tell the sick men and their wives the news. The policemen ordered the two unfortunate ones to get dressed and come with them. The wives could not be torn away from their sick husbands and the sick men themselves understood what was happening and they did not want to get dressed. With great effort, the nurses stood them on their feet. One wife gave her sick husband sleeping pills. The goodbyes among the two couples was heartrending; the policemen had to use their strength to tear apart the people and the two very sick men left for their march to the Angel of Death.

p. 218

There was beautiful spring weather when they left the hospital courtyard for the street; the sun warmed and the two sick men felt better in the freer air and they did not want to meet with death. They sat on the ground near the gutters and murmured: "We will not go there to be shot."

The policemen and the hospital personnel tried to convince them that they were being taken to be enrolled in a summer colony for the sick. But the two sick men would not be fooled; they lay down near a gate and would not be moved from the spot. No one could understand from where they suddenly had gotten so much strength.

Jewish policemen, people from night work and from the artisans' house stood in the distance and with tears in their eyes watched the dreadful scene. The policemen could not convince the two sick men; one of them suddenly began to shout loudly. This sick man had not been able to say any words for months:

– I can still live! – He roared with a weird voice – Tell the chief that I can work!

The terrible shouting echoed through the alley of the "labor camp" and enveloped everyone with horror. At the same moment, shouts could be heard from the distance:

– How long will I wait for the two worthless men?

Everyone watched and saw the guard standing in front of the door, the gendarme sergeant major and two Ukrainians who watched the spectacle and laughed out loud.

p. 219

The sick men were overcome with terror. One immediately took out the sleeping pills from his pocket and swallowed them one after the other. He roared: "Fall asleep, fall asleep faster!"

The two policemen lifted them off the ground and they went with lowered heads quietly and slowly to the sentries.

They were taken into a courtyard and we waited with beating hearts for the shooting, which we heard in a few minutes.

After a time the Jewish policemen came out alone. They related how the sick men had to get completely undressed. Ukrainians chased them with twisted belts. Each received a shot in the head from behind and toppled over to the side, falling as chopped down trees.

Several hours later the dead bodies were taken to the Jewish cemetery.

p. 219

XLI

"The Trip to Palestine"

Shabbos [Sabbath[, the 20th of March 1943, at four o'clock in the afternoon, the chief came to the *Judenrat* and ordered Kurland, the *Judenrat* official, to give him the lists of those registered to travel to Palestine.

The chief looked through the lists and said that he would now put together a new list of the first Jews who would travel to Palestine. This list would contain those who have earned this with their behavior: the doctors, *Judenrat* members, lawyers, engineers and others who had higher education.

p. 220

The chief ordered all men and their wives and children to appear at the small market for the new registration that he would carry out himself.

The Jewish police went to look for all of these people in order to tell them the good news. These families reciprocally found each other and hurried to the lucky gathering.

The chairman of the *Judenrat* and his wife and son hurried to arrive even earlier for the registration. His sister and her child were just able to receive permission from him so that she could also benefit through the merit of her brother and he took her along to the registration. Pohorila, the lawyer and his wife and two children went to the market; after them came other *Judenrat* members, Gitler, the lawyer and his wife and two children, Kapinski, the chairman's brother and his wife and children, Borzykowski and his wife, Galster and his wife and their married son and his wife, Rotbard and his wife and a daughter, Kurland and his wife and daughter, Berliner and his wife, Szerke and his family.

The doctors and their families also hurried to the new registration: Epsztajn, the very nice doctor and his wife and two young boys; Doctor Lewin and his wife, Doctor Winer and his wife and two children, Lipinski, the old doctor and his wife and their son, the young Doctor Lipinski with his wife and his child in his arms. Doctor Kanan hurried with his wife and son, the woman Doctor Grunwald, Doctor Falk and his wife and child, Doctor Praport and his wife and son, Doctor Kyan and his wife and son, Doctor Warmund with his wife and son, Doctor Dobraszicki and his wife and child, Doctor Rozen and his wife and child, Doctor Branicki with his wife and child, the lawyer, Bratman, and his wife, the lawyer Wilczinksi, the lawyer Lampel and his wife, the lawyer Wajnberg and his wife; the engineer, Firczenpel and his wife and daughter and still others who could "obtain permission" to be allowed to take part in the "registration to travel to Palestine" looked for their wives and children and ran to the small market in order that they not be late.

p. 221

At the exit and near the wire fence of the "labor camp," masses of people stood and watched with envy at how the intelligentsia of the city were lining up for the registration.

At the market, everyone stood with their families; each man with his family. The chief went through the market and spoke in a very friendly way and at ease to someone here, there with another one. The chairman became bold because of the chief's friendliness and asked if he should ask his officials to put together a list of those present. The chief answered kindly that it was not necessary – he had a good memory and did not need any lists.

Meanwhile, those who were late came running, but the Ukrainians who stood guard did not want to let them in. The woman dentist, Bresler, made a commotion: She wanted to join her friend. The chief, hearing the tumult, went to the entrance; Mrs. Bresler apologized for her lateness; she had looked for her husband and could not find him. He was also a doctor. The chief answered that it is a great shame, but he could not wait any longer. He was very kindly and ordered the Ukrainians to permit Mrs. Bresler to enter the market. She immediately stood a lucky one among the chosen. Then, the woman doctor, Wajsberg, for many years the director of the Jewish hospital, arrived. The chief asked her if she had children. No, she did not; the chief ordered that she remain. It was already too late, he said. She would travel with the second group together with the current hospital personnel, Doctors Szperling and Wolberg who had to remain here.

p. 222

Then the converted Doctor Kon, who now was called Waclaw Konar, came running; his wife had just now searched for him. However, the chief did not permit them to go to the market. "Meanwhile, you will remain here" – he said – "You cannot leave your remaining Jews without doctors. You will go with the second group."

Those assembled at the market listened to the chief's talk and smiled to each other; they said, "We will travel first." Satisfaction poured over their faces as with those saved from a sinking ship.

Chief Degenhardt looked at the assembled and noticed that they were cold. They were lightly dressed – they had only come to register, for only a few minutes, they were told. The chief went past everyone, looked them sharply in their faces; suddenly his smile disappeared. He no longer spoke a word to anyone. When he was at the end of the row in which he had counted 147 people, he shouted into the general quiet to his sergeant major, Ueberschaer:

– Alle auf di wache! [Everyone under guard.]

All of the assembled, the intelligentsia and educated people, suddenly trembled. They felt as if the earth would suddenly open under their feet and they would slide down into the void.

Those, too, who stood near the wire fence of the "labor camp" and earlier had looked at the "lucky ones" with envy that they would tear themselves from the Germans' murderous hands and travel to Palestine – also these were struck with fear by the chief's four words:

– Alle auf di wache!

Everyone now knew that they were going "under guard," that they were not coming back.

The gendarmes and Ukrainians immediately went to the assembled and ordered them to go. With desperate looks, the just recently lucky people looked at the "labor camps" and were envious of the masses at the wire fencing.

p. 223

The chief stood in a triumphant pose and derived visible pleasure from the hellish spectacle. He remained like this in place until the gendarmes had brought the 147 victims under guard.

In half an hour, a large empty truck arrived and remained standing 100 meters from those under guard.

The people were immediately chased out from where they were being guarded by heavy divisions of gendarmes and Ukrainians. The trucks received their passengers and quickly drove away.

Everyone in the "labor camp" was curious about the direction the trucks would take. They were immediately seen going in the direction of Olsztyn. The Jewish cemetery also lay on this road.

The "labor camp" people looked on quietly. Everyone understood each other without words. Despite their earlier envy of the "better people" who had awaited "a trip to Palestine," now everyone was overtaken by a feeling of dread. The "labor camp," confined in the three dirty alleys, suddenly felt as if orphaned; the educated, intelligent people, among whom there were many who would console, calm and soothe the moods during difficult moments, were no longer here.

The "labor camp" felt as if the murderer, Degenhardt, had chopped off its head.

At 7:30 at night, a group of Ukrainians came closer to the "labor camp" entrance; they were the same ones who had accompanied the trucks.

It was immediately learned that the 147 people were no longer alive.

p. 224

The three alleys of the "labor camp" were full of people. Everyone was out in the street. A sadness enveloped everyone. Not only those who were close to the victims, but everyone cried hot tears. Everyone felt the pain and everyone felt deep grief and perhaps, in a certain way, insulted by the outrageous comedy that the sadistic chief had carried out.

Meanwhile, no facts could emerge because the Ukrainians did not want to describe anything. We only knew that the chief had ordered by telephone that the residences of those murdered be guarded.

The chief immediately came into the "labor camp" in his auto. He himself made sure that the residences of the annihilated were sealed. He went through the alleys and looked at the Jewish policemen with a cynical smile.

The next day everything was removed from the residences and taken to the warehouse on Garibaldi Street. But the chief himself had earlier searched the residences and as the Jewish policemen explained, found diamonds and gold coins and also great sums of money in the residence of the chairman and some other *Judenrat* members, which he took.

Jewish policemen who were acquainted with several Ukrainians received facts from them about how the 147 people were annihilated:

They had taken them in the trucks to the cemetery. The victims were shrouded with a fear of death and did not want to exit from the trucks. They were beaten with rifle butts and tossed down on the ground. The children were placed on one side and the older ones on the other. Heartrending scenes took place at the separation of the children from their parents and this, too, did not happen without beatings with rifle butts. The children were placed near large pits; a machine gun stood several meters away and shot the children who immediately fell into the pits. The parents watched this horrible picture and tore the hair from their heads, tearing off their clothing in despair. However, they were immediately chased to the pits. Standing at the edge, some hugged two or three people and when the machine guns began to shoot, they fell hugging into the pits.

p. 225

A Ukrainian ended his description in this way:

"A mass of people, dead and alive, was found in the pit. Moans were heard; some struck out their hands; others murmured something. The gendarmes placed the machine gun at the pits* and shot into it until it became completely quiet. After this we sat down in the trucks and came back."

On Sunday morning, the 21st of March 1943, two Jews went to the cemetery in order to bury a dead person, who had died in the "labor camp." They saw large fresh pits covered with fresh dirt, without a hill, just flat, even with the level of the ground.

Everything looked calm as if nothing had taken place a day earlier.

*[Translator's note: The author uses both the singular and plural of the word "pit."]

The destroyed Czenstochow cemeteries

INDEX

www.ingramcontent.com/pod-product-compliance
Lightning Source LLC
Chambersburg PA
CBHW050403110426
42812CB00006BA/1791